Hornets in the Office

Marie E. Rickwood

Contributors:
Joy Eckel, Editor
Les Ashcroft, Photographer

Published by:

FriesenPress

Suite 300 – 852 Fort Street
Victoria, BC, Canada V8W 1H8

www.friesenpress.com

Distributed to the trade by The Ingram Book Company

Table of Contents

How far you go in life depends on your being tender with the young, compassionate with the aged, sympathetic with the striving, and tolerant of the weak and strong. Because some day in life you will have been all of these.

- George Washington Carver

This novel is lovingly dedicated to the following people:

My children: Rory for giving me his insite, Michelle for so deftly adjusting my photograph, Derek for his abounding encouragement, Kellee for lending her expertise to the book cover, Roanne for posting on facebook that she could hardly wait to read it and Jill for buying me a book on marketing when my novel began and for telling me my story was credible. It is also dedicated to their spouses: Justine, Brian, Lisa, Harvey, Chris and Stephen.

Grandchildren: Haley, Dane, Kellee, Katrina, Kelsey, Taylor, Shanice, Dilan, Mila, Hannah, Klara, Dion, Lauren, Alexandra, and Robert(Bobby).

Great-grandchildren: Mackenzie, Sydney, and Hayden.

Step-Grandchildren: Charles, Brandon, David, and Sean.

And to all future descendants.

In Appreciation:

Bringing a dream into fruition is never accomplished by oneself. Many people have given me encouragement, especially my late husband, Randy who would have been proud indeed to see the completion of this novel.

My brothers: Dennis, Roland, Alvin, Mervin and Milton, all of whom gave me inspiration in one way or another long the way.

My sister Georgina took time to read the first draft.
I was overwhelmed by the encouragement she
gave me. And my sister, Celine who said, "Good
for you Marie, I can hardly wait to read it."

My daughter-in-law, Lisa expressed faith in my endeavour, my sister-in-law, Molly who shared my dream and my new sister-in-law Pamela who read the first chapter and begged for more.

Many friends have cheered me on to completion, especially Moira Wathen, Arlene Luksay, Helen Varro, Michelle Keenan, Douglas Singer, Alice and Dick Stasuik and their son, Steven, Margi and Bob Hay, and Wilhelm Jotz and his family in Ansbach, Germany,

The final boost came from my friend, Frank Stevens who said, "Many people start a novel but seldom do they finish."

*And lastly a big thank you to my Editor, Joy Eckel who
so deftly pulled the weeds out of my garden of words.*

1

Revealed

Every second around the world decisions are made. Some are big with serious consequence, others small with no major effect on anyone. However, before this day, October 15th, 1971 slides off the calendar, 28-year-old housewife, Elly Thomas will make a decision. It will be neither big nor small but will ultimately have a monumental effect on herself and everyone around her.

At this moment, she's standing before the stove in her modest kitchen stirring the ever, familiar oatmeal porridge while soft morning light filtering through the dimity curtains dances a fire with her red hair. It reflects the chrome toaster on the gleaming countertop, catches the edge of a shiny rod holding kitchen t-towels as white as a clutch of daisies, and illuminates a tile floor so shiny in fact its pattern gets lost in the gloss.

As she stirs, the aroma wafting through the steam fills Elly with nostalgia. A memory rushes in on her herself, age ten sitting at the breakfast table, her mother standing near with a pot of porridge in hand having just filled Elly's bowl. Her mother's voice though stern carries a gentle edge and keeps unison with the large, wooden spoon Elly is swirling through the porridge as though precipitated by it.

"Eat it all up, Elly dear. That porridge has to stay with you till lunchtime. Don't be lollygagging after school. I want you home. Today our lesson is pie-making. And after that, we'll plan dinner together and make sure the house is in order before your father gets home. Above all else you have to learn to be a good housewife, you have to know how bake a decent pie and cook a decent meal. And you have to have the where-with-all to keep a clean house."

Elly's feet had hit the floor earlier that morning before the alarm clock had finished ringing. She had tightened the belt of her green chenille robe around her slim waist and hurried down the two flights of stairs to start breakfast. First, she'd filled the Pyrex coffeepot with water and grounds and placed it on the back burner then set about to make the porridge. She could have performed this morning ritual blindfolded.

Now with the porridge cooked to her satisfaction Elly spoons three bowls to the brim, pops a spoon in each and places them on the small, arborite and chrome table. Milk and brown sugar finishes the setting. Movement can be heard overhead followed by little thwacks and thumping footsteps, her eight-year-old twin sons have awakened. Then a flurry of steps coming down the staircase in double thuds is followed by a noisy rush to the table. Oblivious to everything else, they begin lapping back their porridge as if they had been roosting at starvation's door.

Their father, Vincent, tall and handsome, his blue eyes echoing the color of the military serge he was wearing, followed. Nodding a smile to Elly, he joined his sons at the table. He cupped the tall coffee Elly poured for him with both hands and took long draws.

But Elly's attention was on her sons. "Come on, boys, it's rude to make slurping sounds."

"Can't help it, Mom," said Randall, the elder by five minutes.

"Nope, we can't, Mom," Raphael echoed with milk on his chin.

"Why don't you try putting the spoon in your mouth, instead of sucking the porridge off of it?" she replied.

Vincent chuckled and stood up. Walking past Elly, he rested his hand on her back. She felt the warmth of it. Then he let his hand slide down to give a gentle pat on her bottom before putting his dishes in the sink. Elly watched him straighten his tunic and tighten his belt. She saw his proud jaw and the face of a contented man. Her love for him tangled in her throat just as it had done when they met at the Beale Air Force Base where she had worked as a secretary. Their whirlwind romance ended in marriage and now after ten years of marriage, that loving feeling remained. Elly considered that a gift.

Within minutes and much too soon for Elly, all three hurried off to their day's adventure. She closed the door behind them and leaned against it, feeling the feathery peck Vincent had left on her lips. Her hand went to her cheek, wet where her sons had kissed her. Their footsteps on the sidewalk grew fainter and fainter, and then disappeared entirely. She closed her eyes and thought about the mundane tasks that lay before her: beds to make, floors to polish, dishes to do, bread to bake, dinner to plan, and, oh, yes, those stiff military shirts to iron. Vincent used a fresh one every day, sometimes two. She grimaced and sighed heavily. Resolutely, she squared her shoulders and went to her bedroom and donned jeans and t-shirt, then returned to the kitchen. After cleaning up the breakfast mess, her resolve faded. Slowly, she trudged into the laundry room and yanked a blue Air Force shirt from the big heap, tipping over the basket in the process. She flung the shirt onto the ironing board and plunked the iron down hard on its collar. It wasn't until the pungent scorch of fabric filled her nostrils that she returned to her senses and removed it.

Chastising herself for her lack of self-control, she walked away from the mountain of ironing to the living room window and gazed out at the misty fall weather, not quite fog, not quite rain, just gloomy—like her mood. Never before had she experienced such sheer boredom. The pendulum of the clock swishing back and forth on the mantel was strangely loud and taunting.

She thought about the social life they had enjoyed living on the military base in Northern Canada. The difference between then and now was jarring.

During these past summer months since their spring arrival in California from Northern Canada, her family had set about to adjust themselves to the little town of Summergrove. During mealtimes, they had chatted about the names of the rustic streets that emanated in rows from the town's center. They had talked about the old missionary churches with sandstone walls and terra-cotta roofs bleached by the California sun and beaten upon by the Santa Anna winds—about how they were still intact and in use since the early days of the Spanish missionaries. On outings, they had paused a while at flower-laden parks and at the government offices, reflecting upon the flags that snapped in the sea breeze.

During these excursions, Elly had remained behind. How could they expect her to go with them while storage boxes still formed a wall from floor to ceiling at one end of the living room? She could not rest until all those boxes were emptied, their contents carefully put away. Nonetheless, it had been a good summer, her sons' dark tans proof of the hours they spent exploring the seashore.

When autumn invaded, the twins had settled into their new school easily. Vincent, too, was contented with his new posting.

Why did things have to be so different for Elly? Today, at this very moment, time was standing still. She recalled life when there was always a party or function to attend. She thought about the squadron dinners, the type of party she really loved.

She could almost hear the red-jacketed violinists who had moved around the room with elbows held high and toes tapping, trilling out the snappy tunes requested by guests. She remembered the lovely presentation: a starched white napkin folded into the shape of a bishop's hat and a delicate red rose at each setting. All had impressed Elly, but it was the tiny salt and peppershaker standing at attention next to her wineglass that brought her the most delight. And when the military chefs donned their white hats and sharpened their knives, no luxury was overlooked, no garnish spared. She remembered the succulent shrimp cocktails in stemmed crystal bowls, topped with red pepper sauce. Coq-au-vin or Chateaubriand followed, served with the best wines. Dessert, a rich flambé of cherries jubilee or baked Alaska, brought to the table with fire rising from its center, was the perfect finish.

She remembered it all with a deep yearning, and her large eyes became moist. Closing them, she leaned her forehead against the cold windowpane. For each of those events, she'd sewn a long dress, slim-cut and jewel-toned, that complemented her auburn hair. It was a task she could complete in one evening, but the compliments she received resonated with her for days. When again would she don those lovely dresses, now hanging in her closet? When again would she dine and dance all evening?

She recalled how deliriously happy she had been when they received the transfer to Summergrove after spending all the years of their ten-year marriage in Northern Canada. It was the transfer of her dreams, but now the joy of it had evaporated. She hadn't realized how the feeling of restlessness could grow to such an extent, be so powerful, so all-engulfing. Her chest ached as she prayed for the courage to reveal her feelings to Vincent.

She left her window seat and paced around the house, from one room to another, trying to shake her malaise. She finished ironing Vincent's shirts and attempted several other tasks, but nothing held her interest. When she was hanging the shirts in the closet, something glittery caught her eye. It was the brass buckle of the belt she had constantly worn to the office on base during the magical summer she met Vincent. It was beckoning like a shining beacon in the night.

Maybe that's what I need to do—maybe going back to work will change things.

Once the thought of returning to work entered her mind, she could think of little else for the balance of the afternoon. She knew there was no putting it off any longer. The time had come—tonight she would tell Vincent. She knew he would be devastated and angry, very angry that she wasn't content just being his wife. Nonetheless, the idea persisted through dinner.

Later that evening, when the boys were at their Scout meeting and Vincent was relaxing in the living room with his tea, he looked up from his newspaper and studied Elly across the room. His heart tripped a little at how lovely she was, with her red hair hanging loosely around her face. He had noticed she had been unusually quite over dinner.

"You're not yourself, Elly," he said, eyeing her tenderly while nervously tapping his foot on the carpet. "Is there something wrong?"

"Oh, nothing," she lied, turning her head to avoid his eyes. The dreaded moment had arrived, the moment she had feared all day. Her heart quickened and her mouth felt dry.

"Oh, yes, there is," Vincent insisted. "Something's wrong. Come on, what is it? Spit it out!"

As he leaned forward, a black curl fell upon his forehead and the newspaper slid from his lap to the floor. He didn't bother to retrieve it; instead, he fixed his gaze intently on her face.

"There's nothing … uh … nothing's wrong," she repeated.

"Elly Thomas, don't you be handing me any guff! I know when something's bothering you. We've been together too long—there's no fooling me. What in God's name is it, woman?"

She shifted in her chair, her green eyes welling over, desperately trying to free the words tangled in her throat.

"I'd … I'd like to go back to work, Vincent," she stammered, her eyes cast down. She couldn't bear to see the pain surely in his eyes. As she waited for his reaction, a strange mix of fear and relief beset her.

"What?" he boomed, springing to his feet.

His reaction made her flinch, then cringe in her chair, as he towered above. It was precisely as she had anticipated: he was furious. At no time in their ten-year history had she seen him as enraged, but there was no retreating now.

"Your place is right here in the house!" he stormed. "We need you here—right here is where you belong! I'm all too familiar with what it's like to come home to an empty house. My poor mother was forced to work, out of absolute necessity—as a widow, she had no choice. You … you have a husband. *You* don't *have* to work!"

"It's not for money reasons, Vincent—you know I've never obsessed over money. It's horrible around here! Do you honestly believe this is my destiny … housework? It's different for you. You go to work every day and interact with different people. I only see four walls and rain out the window, day in and day out. I feel like I'm going crazy. Don't you understand?"

"What about our sons, Elly? Have you forgotten about our wonderful twins?" He had lowered his voice, knowing he was treading on delicate ground; however, the black anger remained on his face.

She jumped to her feet with eyes blazing emerald. "How dare you suggest I'm not considering our sons? How dare you suggest such a horrible thing? Haven't I given my entire existence to them, to you and to the house? Haven't I performed all exceptionally well? Haven't I? You keep saying my place is in the house, Vincent Thomas. Well, allow me to enlighten you. My marriage was to you, not to this damn house!"

Sobs accompanied her outburst as she ran into the bedroom. She grabbed a hairbrush from the dresser and threw it across the room. It hit the wall with a crack, its handle snapping in two. She collapsed onto the bed, the hair falling across her face like a shroud muffling her uncontrolled sobbing. But it could not dampen the pitiful wailing that followed.

The sound of Elly sobbing left Vincent shaken, but her wailing sent him into despair. Rushing to the bedroom, he lifted her up and could feel her trembling as he enfolded her in his arms. "There, now, there, now, hush, hush, darling. It's not as bad as all that. Maybe we can work something out." His voice was soft and consoling. He stroked her hair.

Trying to catch her breath, she said, "You're finished work by three every day and could be here when they come home from school. And I could easily drop them off at school on my way to the office." Tears reddened her eyes and clumped her lashes. "They'll always have one of us with them. They'll be just fine."

He handed her a tissue from the bedside table and pondered her plan. His desire for her happiness pushed aside his parental fears, but the other fears persisted, as they always did. Finally, he said, "All right, you win. But if you go back to work, I want you to promise that if—at any time and for whatever reason—it doesn't work out, you'll throw in the towel. I know how determined you can be—how stubborn you are about achieving your goals. And I also want you to promise to watch out for all the cutthroats and backstabbers and thieves out there. Always be mindful. Always keep your guard up."

Baffled, Elly nodded, but she found it difficult to take his warnings seriously—all this mistrust business, always telling her to watch out. She was happy at the thought of going back to work, happy she had finally revealed her feelings to Vincent despite not having his acquiesce. Exhausted, she changed into her nightgown and laid back, closing her eyes and thinking about how she would find a job. But soon, slumber overtook her.

When Elly entered his office for her interview, Land Surveyor Marcel Lamoure was seated at a slanted drafting table positioned near a window busily applying jet-black ink to pale-blue, mylar plastic. Mesmerized by the scratching sound his pen made, Elly watched in silence as he fastidiously drafted his exclusive north arrow. She could see there were forty-four numbered lots on the large subdivision plan spread out before him.

He was slight of build and immaculately groomed in gray flannels and an olive-green v-neck sweater. An open package of cigarettes lay on the table A few moments passed before he finally raised his head. Astonished at the beautiful young woman standing before him, he smiled bashfully and said, "You must be Elly. I've been expecting you."

To her surprise, he didn't ask her any questions but began talking about his children, as though she knew each one. "Do you have any children?" he finally asked, with genuine interest.

"Yes, I do," Elly boasted, making eye contact and smiling. "Eight years ago, I gave birth to a beautiful son. And exactly five minutes later, ditto, I produced a genuine carbon copy."

Her description brought a quick smile to his face. When he said, "Good for you," she knew he was sincere. She couldn't think of a word to say or a question to ask, but the silence was not awkward. Somehow, she knew the job was hers even before he broke the silence. "You'll be expected to work from 8:30 to 4:30, five days a week, and the pay is $300 per month. My girl, Dianne, will be leaving in a couple of weeks. She'll be here to train you. Can you start tomorrow?"

She hurried home to share her good news with Vincent, wondering what he would say. It had been only a couple of days since the scene with him. And now, after her first interview, she'd found employment. Flushed with excitement, she rushed into the house and happily exclaimed, "He hired me right on the spot, Vince! He didn't even ask about my experience, not one word! I sure hope I can live up to it all."

Vincent couldn't help thinking, *A job interview and he doesn't even ask if she can type? There's something fishy about this. I really have tossed her to the wolves!*

The next day, Elly started her training under Dianne's careful guidance. Sitting beside her at the desk as she explained the rudiments of the job, from reception duties and payroll to billing, accounts payable and banking, Elly quickly realized there was much she needed to learn. But she was thankful she had studied accounting the previous winter, a course Vincent had tried to dissuade her from taking and one she had no idea she would ever need, until now.

Dianne continued to train Elly for the next several days in the basics of the job. When she thought Elly had a handle on those duties, she turned to registering the subdivision plans at the County Office. When the training had concluded, Elly felt she hadn't learned very much at all and felt distraught, but she didn't tell Dianne for fear of letting her down, especially when she had trained her so diligently. She did, however, come away with one thing locked in her memory: the importance of registering the subdivisions at the County Office. It represented the successful conclusion of the surveyor's hard work, providing a new legal description that allowed sale of the lots, so time was always of the essence. Large amounts of money hung critically in the balance and that made the owners very anxious, indeed. The two weeks of training had left Elly exhausted, physically and mentally. On the home front, housework was drastically behind and she couldn't remember the last decent meal she had prepared. On the verge of tears, she confided to Vincent, "I don't think I can manage this job. The house is in absolute shambles, and I feel like I'm letting you and the boys down. There's a lot to learn with this job, more than I could ever have imagined. I can't believe how much office work has changed since I last worked! I don't take dictation and use my shorthand—I don't even type business letters."

"If you really want to succeed in this," soothed Vincent, "for heaven's sake, woman, give yourself some time. It's impossible to learn a whole new business in just a few days, but you're a smart girl—I know you'll get it. Don't go underestimating yourself, sweetheart. Remember when I took you to the hospital to have the twins, and you said you didn't know if you could go through with it. You were great all through the birthing of twins, and you've been a great mother all these years. I know you're capable of anything you set your mind to!"

He surprised himself with his response. The perfect moment had presented itself for him to ask her to quit, but some strange wisdom told him to support her effort. "And another thing: there's nothing wrong with the house that a group effort can't fix. Let's assign some chores to the boys, little things around the house that'll be easy for them to accomplish on Saturday mornings. They're big enough now to do more than tidy their rooms and make their beds. Heck, they're almost nine."

"I should have organized things better before I started work."

"You didn't have much advance notice, Elly—only a day, as I recall. Don't be so hard on yourself."

"I do think it's a good idea for the boys to learn to wash their own clothes, now that we have an automatic washer—it's so easy," she ventured.

"So do I - that's a start," Vincent replied. "Tomorrow is Saturday. So, first thing in the morning, let's have a meeting with the twins and talk about the chores, starting immediately with a house overhaul to get everything back in shape. I'll vacuum from one end to the other."

Elly barely heard him; she was thinking about the job. "Oh, and another thing, adding machines seem to be obsolete, replaced by big, complicated calculators. I have one on my desk the size of a small television that actually has square root on it. And everyone calls each other by their first names, even when speaking to the boss. I can't believe all the changes over the past ten years.

"Oh, yeah, they dress differently, too. Employees actually come to work wearing blue jeans, can you believe it? And I noticed girls in nearby offices wearing hot pants to work—you know those shorts with a little skirt over the top. They're so cute! My clothes are from the fifties. I feel out of it, Vincent, like I'm from the sticks, a real country bumpkin!" She looked at Vincent, dewy-eyed.

He shrugged his shoulders.

"So, let's go up to that new mall, my little country bumpkin, and shop. Let's go buy some of those hot pants you're talking about."

That night Elly laid awake, thinking about the day's events and how great Vincent was supporting her venture, how he had verbally capitulated yet her keen perception saw pain in his eyes weekday mornings when she left for work – the price she was paying for her freedom.

She thought about the new clothes they'd purchased: the hot pants they'd started out for, a stone-washed pair of jeans, white walking shorts and an adorable, mint-green, cotton sweater set that complemented her hair. She'd also picked up two books from the neighborhood library about land surveying.

I'll study those books all day Sunday. At least, I'll know some of the jargon, if nothing else. And I'll make up a procedure book to fol-low—that should assist me in learning. Vincent is absolutely right. I shouldn't give up so soon. My working away from the home should be a group effort. We all share in the paycheck, after all. The boys will understand, especially when I explain what the extra money will buy. And learning some household chores will be excellent training for them. They'll have to fend for themselves some day.

2

Power Struggle

"Good morning, dear," said Lamoure, as he stepped from the pool and made his way to the deck table to join his wife, Ann. Beads of water clung to his tanned shoulders, and his beard glistened in the morning sun. He'd concluded long ago, a morning swim was his ticket to good health. He seldom missed it, even during the rain of the cool fall. "Coffee sure smells wonderful!"

"Shhh," she whispered a finger to her lips. "I've been watching a fawn have its breakfast, so adorable. Oh, darn, it's been frightened away!" Lamoure rotated in his chair just in time to see the white pom-pom of a fawn's backside disappear into the lush thicket at the edge of their manicured yard.

"Sorry about that, sweetheart. No doubt, they'll come back. Coffee sure smells good this morning!" he repeated, as he poured a steaming amount from the silver pot.

"Pete's mid-term marks in college, though not high, are consistent," she said about the eldest of their five children. "He phoned while you were in the pool. Brace yourself, dear he has decided to follow in your footsteps."

"Surveying?" he asked, with raised eyebrows.

"Yes, I was surprised, too. But, really—when you think about it—he's always shown an interest in your work, much more than his brothers ever did."

"Well, that's great to hear, I must say. So, he's finally got his act together. Thank God for that! But he'll have to clean up his appearance and cut off that damn long hair if he wants to make any kind of impression with the developers," said Lamoure. His black eyes twinkled as he enjoyed a contemplative draw on his coffee, and she couldn't remember when she'd felt so happy.

"I'm sure he'll cut his hair in time," she replied, reaching for another muffin. "Long hair is like those ridiculous spats were in the forties. It'll pass, dear."

Lamoure muttered, "I suppose it will, in time. But in the meantime, he doesn't have to go around looking like a hippy."

"By the way, how's the new military lady working out in the office?" she asked, trying to sound nonchalant.

"She seems to be managing alright. I had some serious doubts last week, but something has changed. This week she's on the ball. I guess I shouldn't be too impatient—there's a lot to learn in this business." She smiled teasingly and said, "You haven't been known for your patience, I dare say. What's her personality like? I hope she's not as flamboyant and outspoken as her predecessor."

"No, on the contrary, she seems rather timid. But she does work hard, I'll give her that! Right now, developers are coming out of the woodwork. There's someone new everyday with a chunk of land to cut up. Elly has a full plate. I must have a chat with her this morning to see how she feels about the job. I'd hate to see her quit and be left high and dry."

"I hear she has red hair, same shade as mine," she said and took another bite of her cranberry muffin, really beautiful, long red hair."

"Yeah, she certainly does, and unusual eyes. The color is a mystery. I can't decide if they're hazel, green or light brown."

"Goodness gracious, Marcel, they have to be one or the other."

"Why don't you tell me, sweetheart, after you meet her. At any rate, they're not as pretty as yours." With that, he stood up, kissed the top of her head and said, "Well, this isn't getting the job done. I'm going up to change, and then I'm off to the office. See you at dinner."

"Supper tonight is beef Wellington," she called as she watched him walk toward the house, his tight buttocks tucked neatly into his swim trunks. Even though he was approaching fifty, he still was a very handsome man by any woman's standards. She sat for a while, watching the water eddying in the pool, then said aloud, "I think I'll go to the office this afternoon and check things out."

Elly was carefully inserting pages in her red binder when Lamoure arrived and sat down in front of her desk, startling her a little. Normally, he quickly disappeared into his office. "Good morning, boss," she offered, using the name common among the staff. She noticed his cigarette package in his shirt pocket and the smell of tobacco on his breath.

"How do you like your job?" he asked. Before she could reply, he continued, "You've been employed here for about six weeks now, haven't you?

"Yes, today is six weeks exactly. I've worked four weeks on my own, and I must confess, at the beginning, I was totally frazzled."

"You've joined us at a busy time. I know you have a tremendous amount to keep a record of every day, Elly. I … uh … I hope you'll let me know if you get too crowded," he said with concern.

"I'm hoping this "progress book" will help." Elly pointed to the binder. "I can post any action we take on a client's project. It's listed alphabetically and will always be on my desk for everyone's reference." Elly turned the binder around to proudly show Lamoure. "It will be easy to keep up to date. And if you have a question when I'm out of the office, you'll be able tell the client immediately the stage of his survey. I've also left a column for amount billed."

"I'm very impressed, Elly," Lamoure said, as he studied the completed pages. "It's a novel idea. I can immediately see how beneficial this book will be. May I suggest you add one more column, time spent. That will be an enormous help in giving estimates. You can gather the information from the time sheets and billings. Tell me, Elly, where did you find time to put all this together?"

"Oh, I came down a couple of weeks ago on Saturday to set it up, and I've been working on it each day." Her thoughts turned to the sepias in the back room, all awry in their black tubes, the all-important source plans for a proposed subdivision. "I plan to revamp the sepia plans in the back closet into districts and clean that area up a bit, if that's alright with you. They'll be easier to find that way."

"By all means, feel free to do whatever makes things easier. I certainly appreciate all your efforts and especially you coming down on Saturday." He started toward his office, stopped and turned toward her. "By the way, if you ever need to attend to something for your youngsters during the day, just let me know. My wife had teacher's meetings every once in a while when our gang was younger, and no doubt you will, too.

"Thanks, boss! I'm certain there'll be a time when that'll be necessary."

Lamoure returned to his office and smiled to himself. *If ever I had a daughter, I'd want her to be exactly like Elly.*

Elly sat basking in the glow of the moment. She was amazed at how a few words of appreciation could make her feel so jubilant. She made a vow: if ever in the future she became a supervisor, she would always remember the positive effects of this moment. The compliment gave her new energy to give her very best and a dream to make this office as efficient as it could possibly be. Also lying within her was another dream, a dream so deep she could barely acknowledge it: to one day have her own company.

Elly was filing paid invoices shortly after lunch when an unfamiliar voice startled her, "Is he in?" She swung around to see a smiling, middle-aged lady with frizzy red hair standing before her desk.

"Is he expecting you today?" Elly asked politely.

"I'm sorry," the woman replied. "Allow me to introduce my-self. I'm Ann, Marcel's wife."

Elly wondered if it was her imagination or if the woman had purposely stressed the word "wife." Behind the somewhat brisk manner, Elly could see a kind face and a gentleness that only a weathered mother of five could possess. "Pleased to meet you," she replied, hoping her surprise wasn't apparent. She had imag-ined his wife as a vivacious, young blond, not this ordinary house-wife. Nodding toward the closed door, she continued, "There's no one in with your husband," slightly stressing the word "your."

It did not escape Mrs. Lamoure. "Thank you," she replied sweetly before disappearing into her husband's office.

"Hello, dear," she greeted him. "I'm headed for the grocery store to get supplies for my Christmas baking—going to get a head start on it this year and freeze as much as possible. So, I de-cided to come in early for the household check."

"Good idea," he said as he reached for his checkbook. She ran a fine home, and he appreciated her, but he knew she had really come to check out the new secretary. "Well, my dear wife, did you satisfy your curiosity and make a decision?" he teased.

"Decision?"

"On the color of her eyes.".

"Oh, that," she laughed with a hollow ring. "You know, sweet-heart, you were absolutely right. They are the strangest colored eyes I've ever seen—and a little too large for her pixie face. But if I were forced to choose a color, I'd have to say hazel. She certainly does have fabulous red hair—a real crowning glory, I must admit!

"Really? I hadn't noticed."

***

As winter set in, the rainy days of fall dissolved into more of the same, but Elly didn't care. She looked forward to each new day now. She had implemented many changes at the office, not only improving efficiency but also placing her personal stamp on the operation of the business. Being creative, engrossed and challenged was exactly what she needed.

And she had met the challenge of organizing both home and office. Meals were always on time, laundry always done. On Saturdays, she planned the week's menu. And when she baked or made stews, she doubled the recipe and froze the extra. She taught the boys to launder their own clothes, showing them how to separate whites, colors and darks and instructing them to put the clothes on hangers or fold them as soon as they were dry. The new synthetics needed no ironing when taken immediately from their recently purchased dryer. The twins were growing in both mind and body and were happy to help. And Vincent took over washing and replacing the bed linens every weekend. Her working outside the home didn't affect the household in any way. In fact, it allowed Elly to be more resourceful with her time, and it taught the boys and their father to be self-reliant.

The landowners were the big shots in Summergrove. They had the potential for great wealth, and they needed Marcel Lamoure to help them realize that dream. Elly had learned over the past few weeks that as a navigator in the Second World War, it had seemed a natural transition for Lamoure to become a land surveyor. She had also learned that he had been born in Algiers, the only child of a French patriot whose mother was black. Lamoure's mother was a well-bred schoolteacher from England. Professionally, Lamoure was brilliant. He had a way of instilling a desire to work well in his admiring employees, and his clients also appreciated his special qualities. Everyone, clients and staff, referred to him as "the boss."

The Lamoure Land Surveying Company rented three rooms in a large office building: a small reception area where Elly worked, a side office for the boss, and one spacious drafting room. The field crew, consisting of an instrument man and two chainmen, kept the surveying equipment in their four-wheel drives, only coming to the office early in the mornings for their job assignments. Elly saw them just briefly at the end of each day to receive their time sheets and on paydays. The other employee working within the confines of the office was the draftsman, Darryl Simcoe, age twenty-five.

One would consider Simcoe homely, until he smiled. His eyes reminded Elly of varnished raisins, all wise and all knowing. Contrary to the times, he wore his blond hair in a brush cut. Elly gathered that when Simcoe was born into a family of five teen-age girls, his family had celebrated as if he were the first boy child ever. He soon learned that he had only to snap his little fingers to get whatever he wanted. He took tap dance lessons at the private school he attended, wallowing in the applause, and received a yellow convertible from his family on his graduation day. He was in euphoria and henceforth somehow managed to keep his status in wheels.

His family had wanted him to be a doctor or lawyer, but their suggestions went unheeded when his school counselor advised him to choose what he could do best. He finally decided on a career where he knew he would excel: drafting. He could estimate how many lots the developer could achieve from a parcel of land before his pencil ever touched the drafting board. He was clever at drafting and he knew it—he also knew how vitally important he was to the boss. He openly took credit for Lamoure's mounting success, but never in his presence.

As he sat at his drafting table this Wednesday afternoon, Simcoe could hear the boss speaking with Elly. He heard them both laugh. Oh, how he hated the sound! But what he hated even more was the fact that some underling was winning favor with the boss, stepping all over his own importance. *This redhead sure thinks she's the cat's ass. Maybe if I put some pressure on the buggy-eyed broad, she'll leave.*

Elly would have had to be obtuse not to sense his animosity. He was the disturbance in her newly found contentment, but what to do about him eluded her. His demands for her to wait on him, even when she was busy with a client or on the phone, were becoming intolerable. "Photocopy this for me," he would say, while standing in front of the copier, or "Get me that file," while standing beside the cabinet.

She didn't want to risk appearing incompatible by speaking to the boss. And she knew Simcoe was Lamoure's number one employee. He had been with the firm much longer than she, and his ingenious drafting played a vital role in the business. Furthermore, he would be much more difficult to replace. She was also refraining from telling Vincent about her conundrum. She had waited, hoping it would vanish, but it was only growing worse. Now she must.

After the boys left for Scouts that night and she was enjoying after-dinner tea with Vincent, Elly broached the subject. "I cannot understand why Darryl doesn't like me, hon. I'm always courteous to him—I've even bought him donuts for his coffee break, on occasion." She reached for the teapot. "And there's another issue: he's always asking me to wait on him—sometimes, he even interrupts me when I'm speaking to a client. I'm afraid I'm going go blow my stack one of these days. And you know what's strange about the whole thing? He never does any of this in front of the boss."

Vincent's blue eyes softened as he studied his wife. He could see she was troubled, and there was sadness in her voice and the light went out in his eyes. His immediate impulse was to go to the office the next day and punch this creep Simcoe out. *Who does this jerk think he is?* His words, however, were much more rational. Placing his arm tenderly around her shoulders, he said, "Whatever you do, Elly, don't try to make the little bastard like you. Just continue politely doing your job. That's all you can do. He's obviously envious of you for some reason only he knows. Remember, it is his problem—don't let it be yours!

"The next time he asks you to do his photocopying or hand him things, just tell him you're busy. If he has to wait long enough, sooner or later he'll realize it's much faster if he does it himself. You've been enjoying your job. You don't want to blow it all away by losing your temper." He gave her a grin and a broad wink. "I hope there aren't any hairbrushes lying around the office."

His teasing made Elly dimple, and she knew he was right about protecting her job. He always seemed to have answers for her. But their conversation stayed on her mind all evening and way into the night. She knew her self-control was the key issue. *I'd love to tell him where to go and exactly how to get there, but I just don't know where I stand in the office. If circumstances were different, I'd put him in his place so fast his head would spin!*

The following week, Elly was busy calculating a complicated, overtime-laden payroll, when Simcoe demanded she make him a photocopy of the small plot plan he held in his hand. He hadn't noticed the boss standing quietly at his doorway.

"I'm very, very busy, Darryl," she replied, eyes on her work.

"I said, 'Make me a copy,'" he hissed.

She looked up with eyes blazing, grasped the stapler on her desk and was just about to heave it at him when Lamoure's voice interrupted her, "What's the matter with you, Darryl? You're standing right beside the machine! Have you broken your god-damn arm? You make your own photocopies—can't you see the lady's busy?"

Simcoe hurried from the room, his face crimson. Never had the boss spoken to him that way in the past. Back at his drafting table, he pounded his fist on his palm until it was as red as his face and muttered, "Some day, girl, some day!" He spent the rest of the day, while drafting longitudes and latitudes on a large subdivision plan, hatching a plan of revenge.

Lamoure's fury surprised Elly, but it also sent a cascade of relief over her. Thank goodness, he had stepped in before the stapler hit its mark. But Lamoure's reprimand served an even greater purpose for Elly. It made her realize, for the first time, that there's a real power struggle between the sexes in the business world and—more importantly—that she was of equal value to Lamoure's enterprise.

3

Revenge

Weeks and months quickly rolled the changing seasons into summer. But Simcoe's emotional wound had not healed. More and more he noticed the rapport that had developed between Elly and the boss, and more and more he resolved to find a way to discredit the redhead.

"My wife will be dropping by for her monthly check around one thirty today. Could you please have it ready for her? Just put it in the top drawer of my desk. She'll know where to find it if I don't get back from lunch in time. Thanks, Elly," said Lamoure.

"I'm just about to leave for the tax office," Elly said. "I should only be about ten minutes. When I get back, I'll get it ready." She heard the boss coughing as he walked down the hall. Their conversation had drifted through the open doorway, straight into the drafting room and Simcoe's ears.

Elly glanced at her watch. It was after noon—there wasn't any time to spare. She stood up and, quickly turning to leave, snagged her panty-hose on the desk, leaving a gaping hole. *I can't go downtown like this! I'd better take them off. Thank goodness, my legs are tanned—no one should notice.* She put them in a paper bag and set it on the floor by her wastebasket. A few seconds later, she called out to Simcoe through the open doorway.

"Please listen for the phone, Darryl. I have to go to the tax office. I won't be long, only about ten minutes." She faintly heard his mumbled assent, unsurprised by his lack of courtesy.

Simcoe, on his own in the office for the first time in months, pondered his revenge. Suddenly, he had an idea that would cast Elly in a bad light—or, at least, embarrass her. *I'll hide the checkbook, and when Ann comes in, Elly will have to explain. Hmmm, where shall I put it? Oh, I know that old desk.* As he removed the checkbook from the top drawer of Elly's desk, where he'd often seen it, he spied the brown bag on the floor by her wastebasket. Opening it, he saw the panty-hose and thought, *well, this couldn't be more perfect! I'll save them, and when the time is right, they'll come in handy—very handy, indeed!*

Back in the drafting room, Simcoe hid the checkbook in the old desk at the back of the room. Then he stuffed the brown bag into his attaché case, sat down at his station and rubbed his hands together with satisfaction. A few moments later, Elly returned, breathless from her quick walk to the tax department. Before she could remove her dripping raincoat, Simcoe walked up to her desk. "What took you so long? I have to go to lunch. Just take messages if anyone calls while I'm out."

"Be happy to," Elly replied, without looking up. "Better take an umbrella—it's pouring." After he left, she opened the desk drawer and felt around for the checkbook. To her astonishment, it was gone. "That's strange—it was in here before I went out," she said aloud. "I'm absolutely positive it was!" She started a systematic search of her office area.

Then she realized Simcoe had been completely alone in the office. Acting on her suspicion, she moved her hunt to the drafting room. She looked under piles of right-of-way and posting plans. She looked in the sepia-room she'd recently organized and on all the library shelves. The checkbook was nowhere to be found. She all but given up hope when she spied the only place she hadn't looked, the small desk at the far end of the room. Sure enough, there it was in the bottom drawer. *That devil!* An idea took shape as she returned to her desk, and she giggled with excitement as she prepared her response.

A few minutes later, Lamoure and his wife walked through the door, followed closely by Simcoe, who'd encountered them in the hallway. "Looks like we have that doggone rain again," Mrs. Lamoure said as she struggled with her umbrella.

"I got caught in a downpour, too, when I was out," Elly replied. Through the open doorway, she could see Simcoe taking his seat at his drafting table. He was wearing a faint smile of anticipation, and she knew he was, once again, eavesdropping.

"If you'll just give me my check, Elly, I'll get my husband to sign it. Then I'm off—I have so much to do." As she removed her wallet from her purse, a long grocery list fell to the floor.

"Of course, I have it right here," Elly replied and handed it to her. Swiftly turning her attention to Simcoe, Elly saw that he had risen from his desk and was slowly moving toward the old desk. When he opened the bottom drawer, he was greeted by a note in florescent red.

A BLACK CURSE TO THE OFFICE PRANKSTER

Bad luck will come to anyone who steals and hides anything belonging to others! The checkbook has been returned to the rightful owner.

The Office Phantom

Simcoe's face turned white before taking on the scarlet shade of the writing. Crumpling the note into a tight ball, he flung it into the wastebasket, then cast a furtive glance in Elly's direction, just in time to see her turn away. He slumped at his desk, feeling utterly thwarted, until his eyes focused on his briefcase and he remembered his trump card: the nylons. He spent the rest of the afternoon scheming how he would play that hand.

First thing the following morning, Lamoure entered the drafting room. "Elly is going to be busy with me in my office. I've finally completed that proposal for the Department of Highways, and I want to go over it carefully with her before she starts typing it. Please listen for the phone and take a message. We should be finished in about a half hour."

They had no sooner gone into Lamoure's office than the telephone rang. "Hi there Darryl I wasn't expecting you to answer. "Where's Elly this morning?" Mrs. Lamoure asked. Simcoe thought quickly then replied, "She's in the boss's office. They're in there together, the door is closed. I don't want to disturb them."

Mrs. Lamoure thanked him, hung up and continued with her dusting. But the emphasis Simcoe had placed on the word "together" lingered, and the more she thought about it, the more it bothered her. *Could he? Would he? A man is a man.*

It was mid-morning when Elly said she was running out to do the banking and would be back shortly. Within a few minutes, Lamoure said he had to go to the dentist. He was barely out the door when the telephone rang again.

"This is Ann. Can I speak to my husband now, please?"

"I'm sorry, but they just left the building together."

There was that word again. "Well, I'm on my way downtown to share some good news with him. So, I'll just come and wait for him to return." Tucking the letter into her purse, she left the house.

Simcoe hurried into Lamoure's office and positioned the brown bag in the desk drawer, purposely pulling a foot of the nylons out of the bag and leaving the drawer ajar. When Mrs. Lamoure arrived and entered her husband's office to wait, she spied the nylons peeking from the bag and fled from the office, thunderstruck. From his drafting table, Simcoe saw the look on her face and smiled.

When Elly returned from the bank, she sat down at her desk, put a fresh sheet of paper in the typewriter and began to type the quotation given to her earlier. A few minutes later, Lamoure walked in and nodded at her, then went into his office. His open drawer and the brown bag immediately caught his attention.

"Have you any idea where this came from?" he asked, holding up the bag.

"What is it?" He handed it to her, a half smile on his face.

"Oh, my pantyhose! Oh, goodness! They were on the floor by my wastebasket yesterday for the janitor. I should have disposed of them then." She could feel her face burning.

"I don't know how they ended up in my drawer. You must be more careful with personal things like that, Elly."

"Sorry, boss," she replied, mortified. As usual, Simcoe overheard their conversation and said, "Yes!" under his breath. *I wish I could hear what Ann has to say to him when he gets home today. Tomorrow should be a very interesting day in the office—a very interesting day!*

The next day brought no surprises to anyone, except Simcoe. Lamoure and Elly were jovial, and Elly even received a compliment on flawlessly typing the proposal. Lamoure had quickly put his wife's mind to rest with a hug, saying the janitor must have put the bag in his drawer—and that she, and she alone, would always be the love of his life.

Simcoe's disappointment only motivated a much grander scheme, one that would take some planning—one that would place him in charge of practically, if not absolutely, everything.

***

Following the end of the Vietnam War, California's economy was skyrocketing, and developers came to Lamoure by the dozens to cash in on their land holdings. They knew lots would sell quickly at good prices. Overwhelmed by the influx, Lamoure referred many clients directly to Simcoe and hired several more chainmen, as well as Rachel John, a petite blond experienced at drafting.

In the past, when Lamoure needed an engineer on site for road construction and installation of utilities, he'd hired his friend, a civil engineer who rented an office on the top floor of the same building and was pleased to have the business. Simcoe, however, had been pushing Lamoure to hire a permanent engineer.

A breeze floating through the open window of the drafting room and through to the front reception area, a welcome respite from the August heat, blew a paper from Elly's desk. As she was bending to pick it up, she heard a strange voice, "You know, young lady, that's why we have paper weights." Startled, Elly looked up to see a smiling, middle-aged man in coveralls with "Project Engineer" on the bib. The ball cap perched on the back of his head revealed some balding.

"If I had the privilege of Mr. Wind's busy itinerary, I could be prepared. Is Mr. Lamoure expecting you?"

"I'm here to see Darryl Simcoe," he replied in an authoritative voice.

"Certainly, he's in the drafting room. Come this way, please."

Simcoe bounced to his feet and stepped from behind the drafting table with hand extended. "You must be Bill Hauser. I'm Darryl Simcoe. How'd ya do? It's nice to put a face to the voice. It didn't take you long to get here. I was afraid you'd be delayed by those Santa Anna winds." Then, as Elly headed back to the reception area, Simcoe shouted, "Shut the damn door!"

Shocked, Elly gently closed the door. Although she had experienced Simcoe's hostility before, he'd never spoken to her so harshly, especially in front of a visitor. And he knew how stifling her reception area would be without the air circulating. When Rachel returned from lunch and plopped down on a chair in front of Elly's desk, she immediately noticed the closed door.

"What's going on in there, some kind of important meeting?"

"I don't know. A man with "Project Engineer" on his coveralls came in and asked specifically for Darryl, who obviously was expecting him. He shouted at me to shut the door. And very rudely, too, I might add."

"That's so ignorant!" she exclaimed. "I bet if Marcel were here, he wouldn't be shouting at you—or closing the door." She picked up an envelope from Elly's desk and fanned herself. "It's so hot in here!"

"I'm expecting Marcel back from lunch any moment. We'll just have to be patient. I bet you the stranger in there with Darryl is an applicant for the engineer's position. They've had some pretty lively discussions lately about hiring one."

Inside his office, Simcoe repeated, "It didn't take you long to get here. I wasn't expecting you until 3:00."

"I drove all night, wind at my back and eight cylinders under the hood. Thank God, there wasn't much traffic. By the way, who's the classy-looking redhead out front? You know what they say about redheads: a truck driver will stop for a blond or a brunette but will back up fifty feet for a gorgeous redhead like her."

"You mean the receptionist? Just ordinary military trash." Simcoe continued, "Well, let's get down to business. I've been employed with this land surveyor for four years now, and business is really starting to pop! Developers are coming out of the woodwork, so to speak."

Hauser's pulse quickened. "Yeah, I've heard business in this neck of the woods is on an upswing. It's all the talk upstate, my friend, and the reason you're privileged to be looking at yours truly today."

"We're developing large parcels of land, most of it the holdings war vets purchased when they came back from fighting. The rest is farmland easily extracted from the reserve in conjunction with the Williamson Act. All the land is premium property and ripe for subdividing. And the demand for construction is creating a good price for each lot." Simcoe paused and glided behind the drafting table, gesturing. "Here's an example of a subdivision I'm creating." He deliberately had spread out the largest project.

Hauser glanced down at the large drawing and was flabbergasted to see lots numbering in the hundreds. "You mentioned in your advertisement that you need someone experienced in laying water and sewer lines and building roads. Well, look no further—you've just shaken the hand of a utility specialist! I have experience in all of that and more. I've been project engineer for many a large subdivision, not to mention chief engineer for the City of Townfolk. Trust me, I know the ropes!"

"Interesting, very interesting," Simcoe said, stroking the midday stubble on his chin. "There's one little problem I've been trying to work out. The boss is not convinced we should be adding engineering to our repertoire. He has an engineer that's been getting all our work, a friend from Navy days."

"The best approach to winning someone over is always the monetary one," Hauser said. "We need to explain that he should put the engineering buck directly into his own pocket, to hell with loyalties."

"If I can convince him, what's in it for me?"

"Clearly, we'll have to organize a corporate structure. And we'll definitely need larger quarters. But we shouldn't move too quickly. First, let's try to get me on board and form an engineering company. We'll modify the name of the business to incorporate our engineering service. How does Lamoure Land Surveying and Engineering sound? Later, we can construct our own office. I'm experienced with that, too."

"What's in it for me?" Simcoe persisted, his small eyes almost pleading.

Hauser looked down at the subdivision and back at Simcoe. "I see you in a much more important position than what you're doing now. I see you as office manager, coordinating everything coming in and out of this office." He paused for a few seconds and added in a lower tone, "And perhaps, in the future, a partner. You'll definitely be irreplaceable. I'd heard about your expertise as a draftsman long before we talked on the telephone. That's no bull, my friend! Your talents are well known." He looked into Simcoe's eyes, instantly knowing he'd hit his mark.

"Alright, then," said Simcoe, struggling to conceal a smile. "I'll have a discussion with the boss this afternoon. Come around 10:00 tomorrow morning—better still, let's meet for breakfast at the Ritz Cafe at 8:00. I'll arrange a 10 o'clock appointment for us with Marcel. Remember, our agreement must be strictly confidential."

"The secret is ours and ours alone!" confirmed Hauser, shaking Simcoe's hand. "See you in the morning." As he passed Elly and Rachel, he gave Elly a broad wink.

When Elly arrived at the office the following morning, the boss was coughing copiously. "Can I get you a drink of water?" she offered.

"Please," Lamoure said in a strangled voice. He started coughing again and couldn't stop this time. Elly scurried for water and watched as he drank quickly, his hand trembling. He pounded his chest, then smiled at Elly with watery eyes, "I just couldn't reach that damn tickle."

"You don't look too well, boss," Elly commented. His normally tanned skin was pallid and flushed from the exertion. He had dark circles beneath his eyes.

"I've been a bit overworked lately—I understand it's called 'customer overload.'" He stifled a yawn and continued, "Other than a little tired, I'm fine."

"I haven't seen Darryl this morning," Elly remarked.

"He's having breakfast with a civil engineer. I understand he was here yesterday. They're both coming in around 10:00 for a meeting. We'll need coffee, if you don't mind, Elly." His voice lacked enthusiasm.

Simcoe had risen bright and early, showered quickly and put on his best suit. In his mind, he was already the new office manager—and he was dressing for it. Elly had just placed a fresh pot of coffee in Lamoure's office when the two men came through the front door. "Good morning, Elly," Simcoe said, with sophistication to match his attire. "This is our new engineer, Bill Hauser"

Elly was taken aback—not only was it was the first time he had ever said good morning to her, she also wondered how he could be introducing the new engineer when the boss had yet to meet him. She did not have time to respond.

"New Engineer?" Lamoure repeated from his doorway. "That's a premature assumption, young man."

Hearing the edge to his voice, Simcoe quickly capitulated, "I was only joking, boss, but I'm certain it'll be a fact after our meeting."

"Come on in, then," Lamoure said, halfheartedly extending his hand to Hauser before walking into his office.

Taking up the rear, Simcoe shut the door behind him and continued, "Trust me, boss—it's the only way to fly. We need to expand our horizons, you know. Work has really picked up. I have at least fifty new subdivisions, and they all need services. And here's the man who can take care of it for us right on site."

"Yes, siree, Bob, I'm the man," Hauser bragged. "I have more experience in municipal water and sewer lines than Carter has pills! And roads, hell, I supervised the main artery across the state's interior." His chest puffed as he squared his shoulders. Lamoure wasn't impressed, but his back was against the wall. He needed Simcoe, and now it appeared Simcoe and Hauser had become a package. He was just too exhausted to fight.

Simcoe leveled his gaze at Lamoure. "Our revenue will double. Just think what that'll mean!"

Ignoring Simcoe's statement, Lamoure turned to Hauser. "Are you familiar with Summergrove's bylaws?"

"No, but I'm sure they're not much different from other towns in California. I'll be checking that out—you can be sure."

Pleased with Hauser's honesty, Lamoure pondered in silence while the two men waited. When he finally spoke, it was not without a measure of misgiving. "Alright, you've convinced me. But let it be known, here and now, that I reserve the right to revoke our partnership any time I see fit."

"Of course," Hauser agreed, shaking Lamoure's hand vigorously. "Oh, there are a couple of things we should discuss straight off," he continued. "This office space is totally inadequate. I've checked around Summergrove, and the rent for a larger one is phenomenal. I'd be happy to engineer the construction of a new building for us. The monthly cost wouldn't be any more than rent, and you'd have equity."

The ball was rolling too quickly. Lamoure was still trying to figure out how to tell his friend that his engineering services were no longer required—and now this. But Hauser was right: it irked him to write that rent check every month. Maybe the time was ripe to purchase.

"There's an ideal double-lot package just this side of the tracks in the south end. It's an excellent deal—I've checked around," Hauser continued.

"Bring me the details," Lamoure said and picked up his drafting pen to signal the meeting was over.

"Oh, one more small thing," Hauser said.

"There's more?" Lamoure groaned. "It's been quite enough for one day."

"I understand your business is growing by the day. To maintain your efficiency, I believe it's time you hire an office manager, someone to oversee your daily operation."

"Whom did you have in mind?" Lamoure asked, half expecting Hauser to suggest himself.

"Why, Darryl, of course. Who else knows the ins and outs of the surveying business better?"

"Darryl's my draftsman," Lamoure protested. "Who's going to draft for me if he's taken away? He's needed in the drafting department, damn it!"

"Look, boss," Simcoe interrupted. "I'll still be your prime draftsman. I'll draft all the big subdivisions, and I'll continue to meet with clients. We'll hire one or two more draftsmen to help Rachel with the smaller parcels. And I'll be the office manager, overseeing it all!"

Oh, hell, what have I got to lose? If it keeps them happy, I might as well go along with it, the overwhelmed Lamoure rationalized. "Alright, let's get back to work," he said aloud.

4

Power Corrupts

When Elly arrived the next morning, Lamoure, Simcoe and Hauser were waiting for her so they could leave. "Good morning, Elly," said Lamoure, wearing a glum expression and a three-piece suit.

"Allow me to introduce you. Elly, this is Bill Hauser. Bill is starting today as our engineer." Before Elly could comprehend what he'd just said, Lamoure continued, "We'll be out about an hour this morning, looking at some property for our new building."

Dumbstruck, Elly could only manage, "OK, boss." Stealing a glance at Simcoe as they left, she saw his smug smirk. No sooner had they left than Rachel arrived, bubbly as usual. Elly broke the news about the new engineer.

"I cannot understand why the boss would hire a man he doesn't even know," she exclaimed as she hung her sweater on the rack.

Elly shrugged her shoulders. "You can bet Darryl had a lot to do with it. Bill Hauser is loud and flamboyant—so different than the boss."

"And he is one big flirt, too," Rachel giggled. "I saw him wink at you when he left yesterday."

"Yeah, I know. It embarrassed me. And guess what, all three of them have gone out to look at property for a new building."

"A new building, goodness gracious, Elly, things are *really* changing around here."

"We'll just have to go with the flow," Elly said. "Whatever happens happens—that's my motto. Perhaps the influx of business has overwhelmed the boss."

Almost overnight, their new building rose like a monument to prosperity. It was a large, square concrete building with small windows and a flat roof, to accommodate future floors, Hauser explained. Elly calculated it would take forty employees to fill it, as it was.

Reminds me of something one would see in the Middle East," quipped Rachel. "It looks like a box."

The interior was more appealing. "It does look warm and inviting," she admitted, admiring the soft beige and moss green decor. A large foyer, flanked by an office on either side, marked the entrance to a large center area where the draftsman worked. Several smaller offices ran up either side of the drafting room. And at the rear of the building, past the small coffee room, was Lamoure's office, the largest of all.

During the Columbus Day holiday, Lamoure and his field crew moved the office furniture. The following Tuesday, Elly was greeted by a new workstation where her desk should have been. "Is this really for me?" she asked in wonderment while studying the high counter, many drawers and ample workspace constructed of olive green laminate. "I love the color. Where did it come from?"

"I made it especially for you," the boss said, his bashful grin belying his pride in his carpentry.

"Thank you, Marcel! I just love it! And I can't wait to put all my things in the drawers—there's so much more space!"

Later that morning, the boss called a staff meeting to discuss work in progress, primarily the utilities for their largest subdivision. When he declared the impromptu meeting over and snapped his briefcase shut, Simcoe nudged Hauser, who quickly spoke up. "Excuse me, Marcel, but aren't you forgetting something?" He nodded toward Simcoe.

Lamoure paused for a few moments then spoke in a monotone, "By the way, effective immediately, Darryl is appointed office manager. He will be in charge of all paperwork that comes in and goes out of the office."

Simcoe jumped to his feet and shook Lamoure's hand with vigor, proclaiming in a voice one notch below a shout, "Thanks, boss!" At last, the plan hatched three months ago with Hauser had come to fruition.

Elly sat frozen in her chair, flabbergasted. She wanted to vomit. But she tried to conceal her dismay as she turned to Simcoe and said, "Good for you, Darryl!" She wasn't surprised he didn't respond. She headed back to her new workstation, her booby prize.

Simcoe immediately took the left front office and began coming to work in a suit and tie, instead of his former plaid shirt and jeans. He also came to work in a brand-new car. Simcoe had purchased many new cars—a new one each spring, in fact—but this one was different, a black 1973 Corvette. Although everyone who passed by stopped to admire it, Elly thought it looked like a torpedo.

Hauser promptly claimed the office on the right side of the foyer, which gave him a bird's-eye view of everyone entering the building. He put a sign on his door that read, "Engineering Services." Also proudly displayed in his office was a glass cabinet holding his gun collection, an assortment of revolvers, rifles and pistols.

"I sincerely hope you have a license for those things," commented Lamoure, standing in Hauser's doorway.

"Of course, everyone up in the interior has a gun license, and anyone who is someone has a gun. It's the right of the people to keep and bear arms," he grinned proudly having quoted the second amendment. "This is my favorite." He extracted a black 45 with an ivory handle to show Lamoure, who merely glanced at it, grunted and walked away.

New clients continued to come in by the dozens, and it soon became necessary to hire additional draftsmen and experienced field crew. Lamoure could see how busy Elly had become and asked her to come into his office for a talk one morning. Elly wondered if she'd done something wrong, perhaps Simcoe had a complaint.

"With the increase of business and staff, it's become evident to me how busy you've become. I think it's high time we make some significant changes. You do an excellent job with bookkeeping. And now that we've expanded, I can visualize it as a full-time position for you. How do you feel?"

"In all honesty, boss, I have worried I might make mistakes if I hurry too much. I think it's a great idea to make it a full-time job."

"Well, it's agreed then. I'd like you to hire and train a receptionist—the sooner, the better. As company accountant, you'll earn $500 more each month. You'll continue with the company payroll, handle the cash and collections and issue checks for the accounts payable—and you'll report directly to me. There is one more thing I'd like you to do—prepare a monthly profit and loss statement. Do you think you can manage that?"

The conversation lifted Elly out of the doldrums she's been in for the past month. All aglow, she beamed, "Yes, I certainly can, boss. Where will my office be located?"

"Just choose. There are several side offices available."

"Thanks, I'd love the one with the large window next to the foyer. It's nice and bright!"

"So be it," he replied in dismissal.

Elly hurried back to her workstation and immediately called Vincent, "I've been promoted! No, not office manager—that was given to Darryl, I'm the new company accountant. No, my hours haven't changed, only my salary—500 more smackeroos a month. I'll explain everything when I get home."

Then, she made another call, "Hello. Please put me through to job placement."

"Mary White speaking. Can I help you?"

"This is Elly Thomas, accountant for Lamoure Land Development and Engineering." The title sounded so good to her ears. "We are urgently looking for a new receptionist, preferably someone right out of school who would like to establish an office career."

"I have an excellent supply of candidates anxious for employment. What will be expected of this new employee?"

"Typing, of course, and she must be able to deal with the public and work under stress."

"When would you like to start interviewing?"

"The sooner, the better, Mary, I was hoping you'd be able to send some ladies out this afternoon, if that's possible."

"That's fine, we don't require much notice. I can organize a few candidates for you to interview this afternoon. I think three would be a good start."

Thirty minutes later, three applicants arrived, and Elly showed them into a small, unoccupied office to await their interviews. All the while, Hauser, Simcoe and Lamoure were in their offices and had no idea the wheels of change were already in motion. Elly selected Sherry Walken, a bubbly, blond, blue-eyed girl of 19 who was able to start immediately.

Returning to the foyer after introducing Sherry to Rachel and the others in the drafting room, Elly gestured toward Simcoe and Hauser's doors. "When the men are free, I'll introduce you. Here is the instruction manual I've compiled. Look through it carefully. I must emphasize, it will be a considerable time before you're completely familiar. I'll work alongside you, as need be. For now, read through the manual several times—take it home to study, too, if you like. I'm going to get busy setting up my new office. So, if anyone comes in, don't hesitate to buzz me. Thanks!"

Sherry began studying the manual while Elly piled the general ledger, daily journal and other accounting paraphernalia into a file basket to take to her new office with red rhododendron peeking through the window. Turning from her desk to make another trip, Elly encountered Simcoe, planted squarely in the doorway, legs astride. "And just what the hell do you think you're doing behind my back, Mrs. Thomas?"

"Come on, Darryl! Move out of the way, please. I need to pass," pleaded Elly, hoping the boss was nearby.

"Not until you tell me what you're doing and who that strange broad is out front!"

"I'm moving into my new office," snapped Elly. "And the new lady is Sherry Walken, our new receptionist in training." She paused a moment for it to register. "And I'm the new accountant!"

"Like hell you are!" Simcoe shouted. "I'm speaking to Marcel immediately."

When he opened the door, Lamoure said, "I was just on my way to see you. You saved me the trip." He handed Simcoe a memo: This is to advise that Elly has been promoted to company accountant and will be hiring her replacement.

"Well, she certainly hasn't lost any time. There's someone new at her workstation, and she's in the process of moving into the side office. I wish you'd discussed it with me first. After all, I'm the office manager." His face had turned red.

"Well, I'm the owner!" declared Lamoure, tossing his head back and laughing, "Grass doesn't grow under the feet of this little redhead—you ought to know that by now, Darryl!"

Deflated, Simcoe walked back to his office and closed the door.

***

The increase in business continued into summer, and Sherry turned out to be a gem. Although she still required direction, Elly was amazed how quickly she caught on. Each morning she reviewed Sherry's work, since Simcoe was too busy with new clients to pay attention to the ins and outs of the office work.

When not overseeing Sherry's work, Elly was totally engrossed with the crunching of numbers. She sat at her desk in front of the large window with her head down and her hand flying over the adding machine. Her promotion did, however, place her on a collision course with Simcoe.

Despite his title of office manager, Simcoe was feeling left out. He hadn't recovered from Elly's promotion, and Hauser rarely discussed engineering with him. Making matters worse, Sherry and all the other staff conferred more with Elly about client progress than with him. He was all but completely ignored, and he wasn't happy about it.

Although Lamoure was thankful Hauser had settled in nicely and was working hard, he could see Simcoe wasn't happy. He also realized it was a mistake giving him the title of office manager, an appeasement gone terribly awry. But he was still the best draftsman around—and Lamoure needed him now more than ever. And he was having trouble with his health, one bad cold after the other. His rasping cough had become chronic, and he was trying hard to quit smoking. His wife had been on his case about it, explaining it simply was not good for his health. In fact, he had announced to everyone that he'd given it up. But when the urge became too powerful, he'd sneak into the parking lot and light up behind his car, thinking no one knew. Everyone did.

Erupting one afternoon, Simcoe marched into Hauser's office without knocking and slammed the door behind him. "Is there some reason you're shutting me out of the business?" he roared. "I hear you had a bidding session today. Why didn't you advise me? I thought we had an understanding from the onset—you'd keep me informed about the engineering aspects of this company."

"Since when do I report to you? You're not my mother. You're not my employer. And you're sure as hell not my supervisor, thank God for that! Just who in bloody hell do you think you are, Simcoe, marching in here unannounced and slamming my door? I'm the educated one with a degree here. Don't you ever forget it."

"We agreed the last time this happened, you'd keep me abreast of things," retorted Simcoe.

"This is a rush job," replied Hauser. "I tried phoning you, but your line was busy. And I tried to speak to you several times these last couple days, but you were hidden behind your door."

"I know Marcel will be interested in learning about this!"

"Ah, shit, go ahead and tell him. But before you do, take a look at the memo that's been in your goddamn door pocket for days. Quite frankly, I cannot fathom why you have one, Simcoe, if you never check it." Hauser turned his back on Simcoe and walked over to look out the window.

Embarrassed and at a loss for words, Simcoe left quickly. On her way to pick up her sons from the dentist, Elly saw Simcoe take something out of the wall pocket. A moment later, she heard him buzz Sherry on the intercom, telling her to hold all his calls.

Sherry rolled her eyes and whispered to Elly who was standing by her work station, "Darryl's on the warpath."

"I know. What else is new?"

A few weeks passed and all seemed normal, until Simcoe started coming in late each day. This morning, he arrived late, as usual, exhausted from another sleepless night. He knew his relationship with the boss was on a downhill slide. Before, Lamoure had turned to him for advice and information. *Before that damn Elly came on the scene. She's gotten far too big for her britches, that buggy-eyed redhead. She needs to be pounded down a peg or two.*

Elly's day was full and she entered the vestibule with thoughts focused on her afternoon's work. Crossing the reception area, she was stopped her in her tracks by Simcoe's loud voice, "Elly, come in here! I want to talk to you."

What's up?" she asked, hoping the interruption would be short.

"Come into my office, please. Shut the door and sit down. I want to talk to you." He turned his back to her and walked over to the window. She sat before his desk, nervously drumming her fingers. "I've had complaints," he finally snarled. "I've had many complaints from our valued customers concerning your behavior toward them." He swung around quickly and pointed his finger at her chest, his face contorted by rage.

Startled, she jerked back. "Complaints? About me! Goodness gracious whomever from?" Her expression bore a glimmer of challenge, while her sweet calm provoked him even further.

"Customers have lodged complaints about your rudeness … your extreme rudeness … in the workplace," he hissed between his teeth.

"That's simply not true, Darryl. I've never been rude to a solitary soul."

"You can't deny it—several have said it!"

"But who would—"

Before she could finish, Simcoe cut her off again, "As the office manager, I have no choice but to discuss this with the boss." He plopped down in his chair and glared at her. Focused now on her left breast, he continued, "And another thing—Sherry keeps going to you for guidance. I'm the office manager. The books are your job. The boss said Sherry should be conferring with me about the subdivisions, not you."

So that's it, Elly thought, her composure beginning to slip a little. *He's conjured this up. There isn't an ounce of truth in what he's saying. Why is he in competition with me again?* She forced herself to remain calm and let him continue.

A small vein in his temple was twitching. He spoke so low and deliberately, she had to strain to hear him. "If Sherry or anyone else asks you a question about office procedures, you tell them to come to me. If you do, each and every time, I won't tell the boss about the complaints."

Elly had listened to enough. She sprang to her feet, her voice shrill, "I cannot believe we are having this conversation! She stamped her foot. "How dare you fabricate things and then try to blackmail me? Go ahead and tell Marcel. He won't believe you in a thousand years! And as office manager, you should be happy things are running smoothly. If you want to secure the approvals of the subdivisions, attend to the legal documentation and organize all the other paper flow, be my guest. Go ahead, do it and pay the consequences!"

Simcoe's shock was evident. Elly had always been so meek. Before he could reply, she had turned on her heel and left, banging his office door behind her.

Unable to still her troubled mind, Elly had settled on the mindless task of filing paid invoices for the rest of the afternoon. During this time, she resolved to let Simcoe take charge, if only to make him realize the importance of proper paper flow. Although she realized it wouldn't be long before the company suffered, how else could she resolve this perpetual problem between them? It was a milestone for Elly. She had made a major decision without consulting Vincent.

The next day, Simcoe explained to Sherry that Elly was much too busy with the books to be bothered with any other part of the business. So, Sherry should come directly to him when she had a question, intimating she'd be in trouble if she didn't. Astonished, Sherry nodded. However, as the days passed, whenever Sherry approached Simcoe for direction, he'd say, "I'll get back to you." He never did. After only two weeks, the subdivision plans were mounting higher and higher on Sherry's front counter. Elly grimaced every time she saw them, and the clients more than grimaced—they were downright angry. They wanted their plans registered in the County Office so they could begin to sell.

And they had to sell before they could pay Lamoure. This domino effect ruined Lamoure's cash flow. To make matters worse, the backlog put Sherry in such a dither she threatened to quit. The consequence of Simcoe's takeover was monumental. He'd fallen flat on his face.

A drawn and visibly exhausted Lamoure knew something was very wrong with the operation of his office, but he was stymied about how to correct it. As he was searching through a file for a plan, he came across one he'd worked on years earlier for an old friend and fellow naval officer, Alvin Jackson. He used to be a systems analyst—perhaps he still was and perhaps he would have some answers.

5

$\mathcal{D}$iscovered

It had been six weeks since semi-retired Alvin Jackson, accepted an assignment. So, he was especially happy to help his old friend Lamoure, fellow sailor in U.S. Marine Corp likening corporate evaluation to a pocket watch, where everything must work in unison to be successful, Jackson welcomed the challenge. Last year Lamoure had helped him extract property from the Agricultural Land Reserve, and now it was payback time

A robust elderly man with a grey mustache, Jackson moved methodically throughout the office, interviewing each staff member. With a careful study of the paper flow, he easily reached a conclusion. Elly was the logical person to be the office manager, in addition to being the accountant. She should be occupying the front office, directing the paper flow just as she had in the past. Simcoe, on the other hand, should move to an office in the back, next to the drafting staff, and head that segment of the business.

On Lamoure's behalf and paying heed to his warnings about Simcoe's sensitivity, Jackson explained to Simcoe how important his new position would be and how he was perfect for it. Devastated, Simcoe couldn't help thinking, *her again!*

Elly was pleased to receive the title of office manager but not overjoyed. All along, she had quietly believed it belonged to her. *Why should Darryl hold the title when I do the work? And why shouldn't I occupy the front office to oversee its activity?*

But Jackson had not completed his assignment. He had to spend some time with Elly to investigate the accounts. Carefully going over the billing, the accounts receivable and the deposit slips, he noticed something peculiar. "Do you have a record of the total cost of a particular job?"

Elly pondered for a moment. "Of course, for a minute you had me puzzled. I have it all logged in this progress book." She reached for it on the corner of her desk. "I call it my bible. It shows the total amount billed and paid. It will balance to the deposit slips and the outstanding accounts receivable, I'm sure."

Jackson asked if he could borrow the book for a moment and took it into a small private office at the back of the room. The excitement he always felt when he thought he was on to something was building. He snapped open his briefcase and retrieved a list he'd compiled when visiting the accountants' offices of several customers. He compared the totals to the ones in Elly's progress book, examining each one and comparing the numbers. The total job cost from the customer list was much higher than what Elly showed in the progress book.

Returning to Elly's desk, progress book in hand, he said, "This is a very helpful book you have here, Elly. Can we crosscheck the job totals of a few customers against your copies of the invoices, just to verify the totals? We can't be too careful when it comes to accounting. Oh, another thing, you must keep this strictly confidential," he said with a smile.

"Of course," Elly replied with such earnestness Jackson smiled again.

"Let's see. How about starting with the Adam's project?"

They checked three large accounts. In each case, the customer's total cost was higher than Elly's record. In these three accounts alone, the difference was $3500. Something was very wrong, indeed.

"Tell me, Elly, do you ever have cash to deposit? Do the customers ever pay in …cash?"

"Very seldom, actually, I cannot remember anyone paying with cash. Oh, that's not quite true. One did once, and that was for a hundred dollars. We replaced a post on the corner of his property. I can show you the deposit if you like."

"That won't be necessary." Jackson drew his hulk up from the chair, thinking. *It's time to pay a return visit to the customers.* "Thank you, Elly. You've been a great help."

Jackson visited the largest company first and asked to speak to their project manager, John Smith. Extending his hand for a hearty shake, he explained, "I have been engaged by Lamoure Land Surveying to audit their accounts. I've received some numbers from your company's accountant, but I need to discuss something else with you, something very important. I hope you can spare me a few moments."

"Yes, but we'll have to make it quick. I'm expected at a meeting in a few minutes."

"This won't take long," replied Jackson. "When you visited the land surveyor to engage their service, with whom did you speak? Smith rubbed his chin for minute. "That's quite a while ago now. Let me see. Oh, yes, it was a man named Darryl. I remember because I have a son by that name."

"I see," said Jackson. "Did he quote you a figure?"

"Yes, after he quickly calculated the number of lots involved in the project, he gave me a price."

"Tell me, did you give him any cash … at that time?"

"No, but he did ask me to come back the next day with some plans he needed for the job, along with a cash retainer of $1500, which I gave him."

"Would this amount have been included in the total job cost your accountant gave to me?"

"Of course, he would've made a record of it on the cost sheet and in their file when he gave me the cash to take to the surveyor,"

John replied, looking at his watch. Jackson took the hint, thanked him and left. He needed to talk to some of the other customers, the sooner the better. They all told him the same story. His hand was trembling when he finally opened his car door to return home. In all the corporate revamping he'd done, he'd only encountered one other prime case of embezzlement.

This is going to be a difficult revelation to explain to Marcel. And what if Darryl tries to implicate the little redhead? It would be his word against hers. No doubt he'll say he handed her all the money to deposit in the bank. This is one hell of a sticky situation, if ever there was one!

But as sticky as it was, he knew exactly what to do next: investigate one Darryl Simcoe's spending habits. His spending habits would tell all. But not today—he was tuckered. Tomorrow he'd run a personal credit check on Simcoe, confident he'd find exactly what he needed to know. That would be the easy part. Sharing the news with the boss would be something else.

"Good morning, Sherry," said Jackson, dapper in his three-piece suit. "Please ask Marcel if he can see me this morning."

"I'll buzz him right now." Elly walked in just at that moment. "Good morning, Alvin," she said, smiling. Before he could reply, Sherry interrupted, "The boss will see you right away.

Elly watched Jackson shuffle across the drafting room toward Lamoure's office. How she would've loved to be a fly on that wall! She started processing the accounts payable but found keeping her mind on her work difficult. She kept reliving yesterday's review of the accounts, wondering why the customer records differed from her own.

Just as she finished addressing the envelope to the last supplier, Lamoure buzzed her. When she entered his office, he said, "We have to discuss something with you, Elly, something very serious. But first, we want you to understand that it is strictly confidential. Do you understand?" He began nervously drumming his fingers against the drafting table.

Elly's heart quickened a beat. "Of course, boss. I won't breathe a word to anyone. You know you can trust me."

"It appears, Elly, we have a serious problem with the accounts. We need to ask you again, has Darryl ever given you cash, cash from clients to deposit in the bank?"

Elly felt the intensity of the two men as they stared at her. "No, he never has. There was only one time any cash was given to me, and that was by a client who gave me a hundred dollars to put on his account. You'll recall, Mr. Jackson, we discussed that yesterday. All the billing I've done is noted in the progress book, and all has been deposited in the bank. There are no checks left in the building over night. I bank daily. I don't understand how there can be any sort of problem with my accounting." She cast wide eyes from one to the other apprehensively.

Lamoure quickly drew in his breath. "I don't for one minute think there's any problem with what you've been doing, Elly. I'm sure you are doing a fine job. I trust you completely. Thanks for coming in to talk to us."

After Elly left, Jackson said, "So, it appears Darryl has been skimming money from most of the clients. There is a marked difference between what you billed them and what their records show they paid. And as you can see from the personal credit check, his spending habits have put him in a financial crunch. The problem is, unless we do a lot of footwork, we'll never know exactly how much he's skimmed. Just with the handful I've contacted, it's well in excess of $10,000, and who knows how long he's been doing it. Marcel, I think it is time we have a talk with Darryl, a serious talk."

Simcoe answered Lamoure's and came directly into his office., Jackson did not leave any wriggle room. "What have you been doing with all the retainers you've received from the clients?"

"I don't receive retainers," stammered Simcoe.

"We know you have been receiving retainers every time a new job was started," declared Jackson. His eyes darkened in his attempt to ferret the truth.

"Oh, you mean the money they deposit on their accounts," Simcoe replied, trying to sound naive. "I wasn't sure what you meant. I give it all to Elly, of course. She's the accountant." He shifted in his chair, eyes darting from one to the other.

"You've been buying yourself a new Corvette every year," said Lamoure. "Hell, man, even I can't afford that."

"Are you accusing me of stealing from you, boss?" Simcoe asked, his voice pleading.

"No, not from me, Darryl, from my trusting clients. In some way, that's worse. The clients are my livelihood—they trust me. What you've done is unconscionable. Your thievery has made me the most expensive surveyor in all of California! Yes, when you look at it that way, you've not only been stealing revenue from me, you've been stealing my integrity and my goodwill!" Lamoure covered his mouth to stifle a cough.

Before Simcoe could respond, Jackson spoke, "This is a matter for the FBI. They have a talent for getting to the bottom of things ... quickly."

The blood slowly drained from Simcoe's face, and his voice was hoarse when he said, "It looks like I've already been tried, convicted and hanged. I'm getting myself a lawyer." He turned and marched out.

Seeing him walk past her office with his head down, Elly knew there was something dreadfully wrong—he looked absolutely vanquished. A few minutes later, she could hear profane shouting behind his closed door. At first, she thought Hauser must be in there with him. Then she remembered Hauser had gone to the dentist. Simcoe was alone.

Elly decided to seek Lamoure's help before any clients came in and heard the uproar. She was halfway to his office when a bang shook the windowpanes, resonating for a few seconds afterward. She stopped in her tracks, her heart thudding in her ears. The realization of what had happened, rather than the sound itself, petrified her.

The noise brought everyone running into the foyer. Hauser, who'd had just walked through the front entrance, was first to open Simcoe's door. "My God, call an ambulance!" he shouted hoarsely, his face draining. "Somebody, call an ambulance!"

Simcoe's ashen face lay on its side in a puddle of blood on his desk. His eyes were wide open and staring upward. A black-rimmed bullet hole marked his temple, and the wall behind his desk was spattered with blood and other matter. The rebound had flung his arm off the side of his desk. A black revolver with an ivory handle dangled precariously from his index finger.

Hauser recognized the gun as his own and immediately regretted bringing his collection to the office. He wondered how Simcoe had found the bullets he had so carefully concealed in the back of an office drawer. Elly was hugging her cheeks as though she was holding her head together. Rachel was leaning against her, her face pallid. Both were quietly whimpering from shock.

Sherry, who returned from her errands just in time to hear Hauser's shout for an ambulance, had quickly made the call. When the ambulance arrived, the medic took one quick glance at Simcoe from the doorway and went no further.

Lamoure took charge. "Touch absolutely nothing," he shouted in a tone foreign to everyone's ears. "And close the door!" Moving like a robot, he walked to the nearest phone and called the police.

The coroner was first to arrive, followed by four local policemen. While the coroner had pronounced Simcoe dead, the police placed a yellow ribbon around the front of the building. They asked all staff to remain in their offices for interrogation. The investigation and the questioning of the staff lasted for several hours.

After what seemed an eternity, the head policeman took Lamoure aside and whispered in his ear, "Suicide!" He also said there was more work to be done before the final cause of death could be established.

Elly and Rachel were both trembling when they walked out to the parking lot to go home that dismal afternoon. "This has been the most shocking thing that's ever happened in my life," said Elly, dabbing her eyes. "I can just imagine what Vincent is going say about *this*."

"I wonder what's going to happen next," replied Rachel tearfully. "I'm almost afraid to come to work."

And working at the office of Lamoure Land Development the next day was unbearable, the atmosphere hushed and dismal. Lamoure knew he must do something quickly to bring the workplace back to normal. Asking everyone to meet in the drafting room, he said in a solemn voice, "This has been a most unfortunate incident! I hadn't the foggiest inkling Darryl was in such a desperate state. If I had, perhaps I could have prevented it. For the sake of the company's reputation, I am imploring each of you to keep this incident hush-hush. The last thing we need is negative publicity splashed all over the front page of the *Summergrove Free Press*.

"But we have to move ahead, so I want you to put Monday's horror out of your minds and start concentrating on your jobs and the business at hand. Time will be our only friend now. I'm closing the office for the rest of the week and will give you all full compensation for the time you're away. When you return, I'd appreciate it if you'd refrain from discussing what happened with anyone, even with one another. We must put it behind us. Thank you."

He turned and walked toward Elly, who noticed his trembling legs. "Please come into my office first thing on Monday."

Nodding, Elly replied, "Yes, of course, boss."

6

That's Life

Elly was grateful that Vincent had not once mentioned his original warning about all the cutthroats, backstabbers and thieves out there. Instead, he had been his usual supportive self when she'd brought the sad news home. She was filled with fright, relief and guilt. The curse she had left from the Office Phantom was haunting her, as well as their recent argument. She should have handled things differently.

She was also concerned about the effect the delay in registering plans would have on business, primarily the cash flow, and had an idea she wanted to share with the boss. On Monday morning she arrived at six thirty. The office was morbidly quiet, but quiet was what she needed to evaluate the outstanding bills and check the bank balance before meeting with him. However, he was already there, gazing woefully at the unregistered subdivision plans piled on the front desk. Elly went straight to him. "Good morning, Marcel. How was your weekend—or need I ask?"

"As good as can be expected, I wish I could have prevented this terrible tragedy."

"I think it's my fault he did this," Elly lamented. "Two weeks ago, we quarreled. He gave me implicit instructions not to give Sherry any direction about registering the plans. So, I told Sherry to leave me out of the equation and go directly to him. But he gave her nothing but a run-around—that's why the work is so far behind. I should have consulted you about it, boss. I'm so sorry."

Lamoure put his arm gently around her shoulders. "Now, there, Elly, don't go blaming yourself. This had nothing to do with you." His voice was hoarse with compassion. "The man dug himself into a financial hole. He'd been grabbing extra money from the clients in the guise of retainers, money he pocketed. We don't know how long this had been going on—could've been years. Alvin and I were about to call in the FBI, and we told him so just before it happened."

"So, that's why my billing records are different than the clients'! I've been wondering about that."

"That's exactly why. And if Alvin hadn't discovered it, who knows how much more he would have skimmed. I'm just sorry Darryl resorted to killing himself. His family is devastated, especially his mother. She told me they've been worried about his mental health for a long time. She said he's been acting strange since he broke off his engagement with his girlfriend."

Elly closed her eyes and thought of her sons. "Oh, his parents must be so sad! "Then Lamoure pointed at the heap of unregistered plans. "Now, what are we going to do about this mess?"

"I'll help Sherry get them all registered. I don't mind working on the books at home for a while, until we take care of this backlog. Oh, by the way, boss, I have an idea I'd like to share with you."

"Go ahead."

"Well, we bill our clients at least fifty thousand dollars a month. If we were to add a 2 percent administrative charge to each bill, we would realize an additional thousand dollars or more a month. We do a lot of legal-type work for clients, saving them huge legal fees, and I'm certain they all appreciate it. I'm certain, too, Marcel, they would barely notice it since the individual amounts would be negligible. But put all together, we'd have enough for our mortgage payment."

"Damn good idea! Let's go for it." With half a smile, the boss headed toward his office.

***

Simcoe's suicide slipped into the unspoken past as the months passed. Lamoure had been overjoyed to have his eldest son, Pete, take over Simcoe's position. But this Monday morning, the boss asked Elly to bring in the age listing so they could discuss the financial papers and accounting reports she had produced. The lack of cash flow continued to be a concern. "There are an awful lot of accounts ninety days old," he noted.

Elly reassured him, "We have them all registered now and should be receiving payments on these older accounts very soon. I plan to start phoning everyone today. By now, most of their lots have hit the market." Determined, she set about calling clients for payments. But she had little luck. Most of them were waiting for their lots to sell and couldn't settle their accounts before. She was crestfallen.

The next day, after preparing a bank deposit for the small amount of cash that did come in, Elly hurried off to the bank. She had grave concerns about meeting payroll. While walking along the quiet street to the business center, the beauty of the budding spring helped dispel her malaise. She paused at the gardens of City Hall to admire the unfolding buds and, as she raised her eyes, saw Lamoure's client Jim Morro approaching.

He was the mastermind of one of the largest subdivisions they had completed. It was a section of land inherited by the five Morro brothers, but now a feud among them had stalled signatures, and Lamoure had not been paid. Elly hadn't been able to reach him yesterday and had been planning to call when she returned to the office. *I'll ask him right now!* she thought as she watched him approach. Even from a distance, she could see him leering at her.

"Well, fancy meeting you here, sweetheart!" he bellowed, his yellow teeth appalling. "Did the boss man actually allow you out of his inner sanctum?"

"Hello, Mr. Morro," Elly replied, forcing a smile. "Isn't this just such a beautiful day? I'm glad I've bumped into you. I—

You can bump into me any time your little heart desires, sweetheart," he interrupted.

Elly struggled to pretend she didn't hear his lewd comment. "I'm hoping you're in a position to pay something on your account. It has climbed up to the ten-thousand-dollar mark."

"I can be in any position you want me in," he quipped, Elly stymied for a response. But then he pulled a wad of money out of his overall pocket and, more than Elly had never seen. "Hold out your hand, lovely eyes," he said and started counting out hundred-dollar bills. "My idiot brother finally agreed to sign."

"Great," she said in disbelief, quickly adding, "No need for you to make a trip to the office, I can just pop your receipt into the mail."

"You betcha," he said, giving her an exaggerated wink and continuing on his way, leaving a trail of raucous laughter behind.

Feeling sullied from the encounter and a prime target for a mugging, Elly stuffed the wad into her purse and hurried to the bank. She knew Lamoure would be overjoyed. Returning to the office and hurrying toward his door, Rachel stopped her. "If you're looking for the boss, he's at the doctor. He said he wouldn't be long."

Elly spent the rest of the afternoon writing checks for suppliers, waiting patiently for the boss to return. But he never did, nor did he call, much to her astonishment.

The next day started normally. Hauser stood before his desk, whistling a Frank Sinatra tune while studying a waterline layout plan. Rachel worked at her desk, calculating hectares of the lots on a large subdivision. Pete sat in Simcoe's old office, analyzing the 10 percent road frontage of a new proposal. Sherry stuffed blue Mylar into the printing machine, preparing subdivision plans for registration in the County Office... And the boss was behind his closed door. Elly, totally engrossed in the numbers game, was working on the financial statements for the end of April. She barely heard Lamoure page Pete to come into his office.

But Rachel's voice was much louder as she stood in the doorway, "Can I see you for a moment, please?" "Of course," replied Elly, cheerfully. "Come in, Rachel."

"I'll only be a moment. If you're free, I'd like to have lunch with you today. I have something very important to tell you. I just can't put it off any longer. "Of course, do you have a special restaurant in mind? I'm easy."

"Let's try Jenny's, next to City Hall. It's quiet, plus her sandwiches are quick and the soup is delicious!"

"OK, Jenny's it is. But first I have to go to the bank. I'll see you there about quarter after twelve."

A few minutes later, a slamming door made Elly jump in her chair. Before she could get up, Sherry burst into her office, crying. Elly moved quickly to her. "Sherry, what on earth's the matter?"

"I was going to get Marcel's signature on a letter, and I honestly thought I heard him tell me to come in. I didn't know Pete was in there with him. So, I went in. And Pete, the big bully, shoved me out so fast I almost fell down." She sobbed again and continued, "Then he slammed the door in my face. I don't deserve to be treated that way. I work hard around here!"

Elly offered a tissue. "Of course, you work hard, Sherry," she said, placing an arm around her. "Marcel has commented several times about the wonderful way you handle your position." She saw Sherry brighten somewhat—everyone wanted to please the boss. "This company couldn't operate without someone like you taking care of the registrations. Keeping that front desk running smoothly is a feat in itself." Elly could feel her dander rising. "I'll get to the bottom of this—you can count on that! In the meantime, go back to your desk and continue with the same fine job you've been doing."

Elly couldn't remember when she'd felt so disgusted. She marched across the drafting room, her anger mounting with each step. By the time she reached Lamoure's office, she was livid, proclaiming in a shrill voice that dripped with anger, "Pete has until noon to apologize to Sherry. And if he doesn't, you can consider this my notice."

When Lamoure realized what had caused her fury, he covered his face despairingly. Finally, he lowered his hands to his lap, but he couldn't stop their trembling. "Elly," he pleaded, tears in his dark eyes, "please, don't do anything rash. When Sherry came in, I'd just given Pete the worst news any man could possibly give a son. He was only reacting to what I'd just told him."

The boss broke into a coughing spell and averted his eyes before continuing, "I can't break the news to the office staff yet because not all my children have been informed. After I tell you, I want you to explain to Sherry and apologize for Pete, but please tell her it's confidential. You see, Elly, I have only six weeks to live. I have advanced lung cancer. All along, I thought it was just a smoker's cough, but I should have listened to Ann and gone to see about it sooner. Apparently, it has been progressing slowly over several years. I tried to quit smoking but … but not hard enough." He released a long shaky sigh.

Elly stood dumbstruck, studying him as if seeing him for the first time. *Why hadn't I noticed?* His face was thinner, his cheekbones more pronounced, and gray had invaded his jaunty little beard. He appeared much older than his 57 years and very ill, indeed. With all anger punched out of her, she whispered, "I'm so sorry, Marcel." She kissed him lightly on his furrowed brow and continued in a husky voice she didn't recognize as her own. "I'll explain it all to Sherry. I'm so sorry, Marcel!"

"So am I," he said. "So am I." Then he swung his chair around to face his drafting table again, unable to bear the tears he knew would be in her eyes.

Elly walked back to her office, her throat so constricted she could hardly breath, she called Sherry in. "Sherry, what I'm about to tell you is in the strictest confidence—probably the biggest secret you'll ever have to keep in your life! Before I tell you, promise me you won't tell a soul."

"Sure, I promise!" Sherry replied, bright-eyed and anticipatory but after Elly explained everything her jaw dropped. "Do you actually mean Marcel is going to die in six weeks? I don't believe it!" Her eyes began to brim over.

"Yes," said Elly, "I realize it's hard to comprehend, but I'm afraid it's true. Just remember he's asked us to keep it confidential until all his family is informed. Please, Sherry, I'm trusting you'll continue doing your job exactly as you have in the past. We must maintain the office, especially now. It's going to be very difficult for all of us." Sherry acknowledged in a small voice, "I understand," then left Elly's office with her head down.

Elly closed the door and mechanically walked to the window. *Will he suffer long? How long will he be able to work, and who will take over after he's gone? How is Ann taking it? And the children, the poor children, they loved their father so! He will never realize the fruits of his labor, retire and enjoy that special time with his wife. And he'll never live to see his grandchildren. Damn those cigarettes!* She left the window, laid her head on her desk and wept.

It was precisely 12:15 when Elly walked into Jenny's. She'd give anything to have cancelled. How does one pretend all is right when the world has just crumbled? She spotted the top of Rachel's blond head in a back booth. *I can't let Rachel know something's wrong. I hope she doesn't notice I've been crying.* "What's Jenny's special today? I didn't notice on the board when I came through," Elly said, desperately trying to sound cheerful

"Hope you don't mind," replied Rachel, "I took the liberty of ordering—tuna salad sandwiches and soup of the day, I believe, vegetable—her vegetable is always good, nice and thick. We don't have much time, and you know how time flies when we start chatting."

"Sounds wonderful, how did you know that's my favorite?" Elly replied, genuinely surprised. She studied Rachel's flushed face. She seemed elated, her eyes bright.

Rachel spoke in a soft voice, "I've been dying to tell you for some time now. It's kind of a long story. You'll recall when I started work, I told you I was unable to have children. Well, a few months back, my doctor told me about another doctor, who was very successful with a certain medication."

"So, now there is a chance for you to get pregnant, if you're of a mind to?"

"Yes!" Rachel replied breathlessly. "Yes, I've always wanted children. I've always yearned to be a mother!"

Elly had never seen a face so radiant, and it slightly warmed her grieving heart. "That's wonderful! Now you always have the possibility, and that, in itself, is something nice to know." Elly recalled the time Rachel had said she could barely look after herself, let alone a child. Nevertheless, she had no intention of dampening Rachel's apparent joy. "You are getting close to 36. Father Time is skipping down the road rather quickly."

"He can skip all he wants. I'm already pregnant! I'm in my second trimester—three and a half months. It worked immediately—first kick at the can. And I've never felt better in my life!" She sat in absolute triumph, awaiting Elly's response.

"Oh Rachel, how wonderful for you, there's nothing in the world more joyous than a child!"

"I can work another three months, then I plan to be a 'stay-at-home-mom.' Please keep it a secret. I don't want Marcel or anyone else at work to know about it, not just yet, anyway."

"Your wonderful secret is as safe as Brinks with me. Mum's the word!"

"Was that supposed to be a play on words?" Rachel laughed.

Elly's large eyes started to brim over. She dabbed them with a tissue, cleared her throat and said, "I don't mean to be such a crybaby—it's just such wonderful news!" But it was bittersweet for Elly. She had learned of impending death and impending birth all on the same day, both ends of life's spectrum and both uncanny as it was, sworn to secrecy.

Later that day, Vincent once again cradled his sobbing wife in his arms and consoled her, "That's life, Elly, that's life. We never know what the future holds. It's always a big mystery, and I sincerely believe it's better that way. We have to keep moving ahead, allowing time to pass. You'll see—eventually, it will take today's sorrow with it. We have to live for today and tomorrow. Yesterday is gone forever!"

There had been times Elly considered Vincent's philosophy on life just so much rhetoric. But today, his words were like a warm blanket. He was there for her, always there to comfort and protect her.

7

Endings and Beginnings

Taking Vincent's advice, Elly kept busy. There was plenty to do. Lamoure was a tidy man and wanted his affairs in order, asking Elly to transfer all his accounts, including those in Switzerland, to his wife before he died. He came into the office for half days for about two weeks, but then was too weak to come at all. His absence left a void felt by all.

A month later, the boss was in the hospital. When Elly arrived, she found his wife stroking his head, as he lay gasping, unconscious on the bed. As a well-trained nurse, she had been able to provide excellent homecare up to this point. She spoke of their romance and their life together, while Elly listened intently, hoping it was therapeutic for her to reminisce. After an hour, Elly bade them farewell and went home to Vincent.

The next morning, Mrs. Lamoure rushed into Elly's office with arms outstretched, sobbing, "He's gone, Elly! He's gone!" They clung to each other and cried.

Now, Elly had much more work to occupy her time. She closed all his personal bank accounts. She arranged for certified copies of his death certificate to finalize his life insurance and pension funds. She carefully wrote a factual summary of his life—nothing flowery, just as he would have liked it—and requested it be published, not in the obituary column, but on the front page of the local newspaper. The caption for his photo read, "Summergrove loses Top Surveyor at Age 57."

Lamoure's funeral, like him, was quiet and dignified—no speeches. The eulogy delivered by the undertaker was a repeat of the newspaper article. After the service, Mrs. Lamoure announced that it was the boss's wish the Christmas party planned for December 15 not be cancelled. He wanted everyone to attend and celebrate for him.

Now, Elly threw herself into preparing for the Christmas party, spurred on by the thought it would be for Marcel. She recalled Mrs. Lamoure saying how much she regretted not having a formal portrait of Lamoure and also recalled that Summergrove boasted a world-renowned portrait artist, Joseph Kovacs, an immigrant from Hungary who knew Lamoure quite well. It would be wonderful if they could present a painting of the boss to the family at the Christmas party. Excited by the thought, she consulted Pete, who agreed and said he would keep it confidential. "Find out what it will cost," he suggested, "and get back to me."

Elly wasted no time in calling Kovacs, who consented in broken English and added that he would need some snapshots of Lamoure for reference. Reminding Elly he was the best portrait artist in the world, he announced it would cost sixteen hundred dollars, cash in advance. Downcast, certain Pete would consider the price exorbitant. Elly was astonished when he replied, "Let's go for it! After all, none of us would be employed here if it weren't for him."

When the artist arrived at the office to pick up his payment, Elly was surprised at his advanced years and the length of his beard, which looked as if it hadn't seen scissors for years. He told her, in his sketchy English, the picture would be ready to be picked up at his home three days before the party. Elly spent her spare time in the intervening few weeks attending to other details for the party. She phoned all past employees, consulted with the chef on the choice of food, and made certain the music was in place.

Finally, the day arrived to pick up the portrait. As she turned into the secluded driveway of the Kovacs' small log home, she worried, *What if the picture doesn't look like Marcel? What if it doesn't do him justice? What if it's a grotesque caricature? It will be extremely difficult to get the money back if we don't like it.*

Flagstones led to the front door, where a large wooden palette with splotches of color around its perimeter read, "Kovacs/Artist." The door was opened quickly after Elly's ring by a short, plump, blond woman, obviously much younger than the artist. "Velcome, velcome," she said. "Yosef vill be vit you in a minute. Come in! Come in! I am Helena, Yosef's voman."

Elly followed her up the steep stairs into a large open area— living room, dining room and kitchen combined. Massive landscape paintings hung all around the walls, one more beautiful than the other. But the one directly over the fireplace captivated Elly, a life-sized nude of Helena stretched out on a velvet chaise lounge. Although painted when the woman was much younger, the likeness was astonishing, quelling her fears somewhat. Her attention was distracted when a gruff voice called out from a nearby room, "Tell young lady to go into my studio. I vill join her in minute."

Elly followed Mrs. Kovacs into the studio and her heart fell. Several easels held paintings of Lamoure, half-drawn, half-painted, and even more were piled on the floor and leaning against the walls. *He couldn't do it!* Elly was filled with overwhelming despair. "Vell, vat you tink? Vich von you like best?" Kovacs asked in a gruff voice from behind her. Then he laughed heartily and said, "You tink are all I have done? No, no, my little redhead! Come into bedroom. I have by open vindow so it can dry in sunshine."

She followed him down a long hallway into the bedroom, where an easel by the window held the finished portrait. He had captured Lamoure's fundamental nature perfectly: dark eyes with honest directness and a bashful half-smile. Elly felt she could reach right out and touch him. Turning to face the smiling artist, she spontaneously embraced him with such fervor he almost fell backward. Righting himself, he grinned and puffed his chest. "I de best, ya?" His wife stood proudly by, nodding in agreement.

You certainly are! Without a doubt, you are! We would be honored if you and your wife would attend the party—it would be most fitting if you unveiled the portrait. Do you think you can make it? Elly could see the fierce pride in their smiling faces and knew their answer before Kovacs turned to his wife and received her nod. "Ya, ve vould be happy to come!" he assured her.

With the painting on the back seat, she started back to the office, driving slowly to avoid bumping it around. Checking the rearview mirror to be sure she wasn't in anyone's way, she was shocked by the sight of the boss smiling at her. Starting, she swerved off the road and came to a sudden stop in the ditch, jarring the picture to the floor. Her heart was pounding in her ears, and an eerie feeling engulfed her. After a few moments, she stepped out of the car and checked the portrait, relieved to find it had not been damaged. This time, she turned it around so it faced the back. She couldn't help wondering if the incident was a sign not to linger in the past, but to move ahead and deal with the future. Just as Vincent had said, life goes on. But she decided not to tell him about what had happened.

At the party three days later, the artist, his wife at his side, proudly unveiled the painting before all the family and staff members, their applause music to his ears. Mrs. Lamoure, teary-eyed but composed, rose and declared, "Well, I finally have my portrait of Marcel. Thank you very much!"

Turning to Rachel next to her, Elly noted regretfully, "This is the first company party without Marcel."

Rachel nodded toward the portrait and said, "Somehow, in a mystical way, he is here, Elly."

Elly agreed and contemplated life's ironies. In the eight years since she had started working again, two lives had ended and a new one had started, all within one small office. She had grown immeasurably from witnessing life at its rawest. Now, she felt there couldn't be anything in her future that would daunt her, a feeling that liberated her.

***

There are good times and bad times in the business world. And in the spring of 1980, Summergrove and most of California was experiencing the worst in history. The recession hit the entire town, but land surveyors and their spin-off trades—builders, civil engineers, carpet layers, painters, plumbers, supply stores and all the others whose services intertwined—received the hardest blow. Without clients, they were forced to look for work elsewhere, many traveling up the coast of California in search of new prospects.

Lamoure Land Development Company was down to bare bones, with small posting and certificate of location jobs the only work coming in. There were no subdivisions to design or roads to build, so Pete had to lay off many of the staff, including Bill Hauser. Elly was upset, but Hauser had reassured her, "Don't worry about me! Are you forgetting I'm one of the best engineers this side of the Rockies? I'll find work, yes, siree, Bob!" And with that he was out the door.

Jerry Easton, Pete's new partner, was like a fresh breeze in the office, his ear-to-ear smile contagious. In sharp contrast to Pete, Easton was a people person, filling the void Pete's technical expertise could not. They and the one-man crew took care of whatever business trickled in, while Elly sat at the workstation the boss had built, primarily making collections calls for outstanding accounts receivable.

When Pete and Easton weren't out surveying, they spent their time in the office behind closed doors, discussing how to keep the business afloat. Elly felt left out when Easton and Pete held these private planning sessions, their secret murmurings just a few feet from where she sat. But what was she to do? They were the bosses.

The hand-to-mouth existence of Lamoure Land Surveying continued as another spring became summer. Cash flow, which depended almost entirely upon the collection of outstanding accounts, was almost nonexistent. Just meeting payroll for the small staff was a feat. One morning, Pete and Easton called Elly into their inner sanctum to discuss her salary.

Easton explained what she already knew: there simply wasn't enough money for her to continue receiving the same salary. "In fact," he said, "we all have to take a reduction if we're to continue."

"I understand we must do what's necessary. It's bound to improve in due course," Elly agreed, attempting to put a hint of joviality in her voice.

"Good girl!" Easton responded.

"Good boys," she countered.

"OK, then, Elly," said Easton, "next payday take two hundred dollars off all three of us. We'll realize a savings of twelve hundred dollars each month, which we can use to pay the mortgage and utilities. Keep deducting it until I advise you to cease."

"Will do," she replied and went back to her desk to ponder her new financial situation. She recalled the labor relations course she'd taken where the teacher said, "You always give to employees and never take anything away." Apparently, he was wrong. There were times when it was necessary. She wondered what Marcel, who had been so ready and spontaneous about giving her raises, would have done during this time of crisis

The following month, there was a small breakthrough. Elly, through a small claims action, settled a twelve-hundred-dollar account. The bosses seemed extremely pleased when she told them the good news. But when she was preparing the next payroll, Easton handed her a note that read, "Give Pete and Jerry a bonus this paycheck of $600 each." It was exactly the amount that had been deducted from everyone's pay. Not only did they get their reduction back, but hers, as well.

Her spine stiffened as she concluded that the cutback had just been a way to cheat her. *What else could it be? They want me to leave, and neither has the courage to tell me. Well, I'll put them both out of their misery—I'll quit, just as soon as I find another position!*

The following week, Elly responded to a small ad in the classified section of the *Summergrove Free Press* that read, "Office manager wanted - must be familiar with all aspects of running an office. Drop off resume at the laundry department of The Summergrove Convention Center no later than April 1."

A few days later, she received a call from a Mr. Stewart, asking her to come for an interview the following day. On her way home, she stopped at the library and borrowed a book on laundries and another on convention centers. Although tired, she read through them in bed, and then lay sleepily thinking about what constituted a successful interview. Her plan was to let Mr. Stewart carry the conversation, but when the time was just right, she would ask a few pertinent questions. She arrived at the office at 7:30 A.M. the next day and attended to a number of small tasks before announcing to Easton and Pete that she had an appointment. She knew they would assume it was the dentist or doctor. She needed to keep her hand close to her chest until she had a job offer.

8

Starting Over

At the rear of the convention center, the parking lot of Sunshine Linen was filled not only with cars, but also with potholes. As she carefully backed into the only spot remaining, she chose to ignore the man standing a few feet away, frantically flailing his arms, clearly hell bent on directing her into the parking spot.

This annoyed her far more than the potholes—one more reminder that, although women now represented a quarter of the driving populace, a lot of men felt women should not be driving—and definitely not backing into a tight spot. In this budding era of the workingwoman, she was grateful not to be among those forced to ride the bus, waiting on the street in all kinds of weather.

On the back wall of the building, a large steam tunnel spewed clouds of wet heat. *What a comedown—going from a land development company where I dealt with some of the town's most affluent to a crummy laundry with potholes in the parking lot!* Nonetheless, her heart quickened when she checked her watch and saw it was two minutes to 9:00. Being late, with jobs still in such short supply because of the recession, was not an option. She smoothed her rust linen skirt, squared her shoulders and started across the parking lot. There were no butterflies in her stomach this time. She was not the same insecure lady who'd applied at Lamoure's.

As she approached the front door, she found her path blocked by a van unloading a hotdog machine with "Sammy's Smokies" on the side. A short, plump man wearing sunglasses approached her shyly. "My apologies, madam," he said. "I hope I'm not holding you up too long. I'm running late this morning—ran into a traffic jam. If I don't have this thing fired up for the eleven o'clock rush hour, I'll miss the early shift crowd. I don't mean to brag, but everyone loves my smokies!"

"I'm certain they do! I'll come by sometime and sample them—perhaps take some home to the hungry men at my house. I hope you have a fabulous day and sell a bundle!" she called out as she walked around the van.

Elly was surprised at the elegance of the Summergrove Convention Center lobby. A crystal chandelier sparkled in the middle of the room above an arrangement of lilies in a huge brass urn. Crimson velvet draperies at the tall windows fanned out on the gleaming oak floor, and Elly admired how the various Persian carpets picked up the rich color. Exquisite local pottery in a glass case that ran the length of one wall, vibrant oil paintings in heavily carved oak frames and leather lounging chairs invited patrons to sit and relax a while.

As Elly moved toward the front desk, she marveled at one painting in particular, amazed how the artist had depicted a seaside that actually looked wet. She'd read somewhere that a renowned local artist had recently donated them. She wondered if the artist knew Kovacs and made a mental note to follow up later. "I'm looking for the office of Sunshine Linen," she told the clerk.

"Just follow that hallway and take the first door on your right," he said and gestured to the other end of the lobby.

The door opened into another hallway, the dank odor of scorched fabric and bleach filling the constricted area. Covering her mouth with her hand, she tried not to breathe as she ventured in. Just as she was about to turn around and run back, a door at the end of the long passage came into sight. Approaching, she saw that it had a sliding glass window with a "No Help Needed" sign in the middle. Through the window, she could see several office people working. A young receptionist seated near the window swept it open with such force that Elly jumped back.

Smirking, the receptionist said, "You must be Elly Thomas. I believe Mr. Stewart's expecting you." Languidly unlocking the door, she turned to guide Elly through the office, swaying her slim hips at each step. As they passed the line of tall, metal file cabinets that divided the room, a single desk on one side and two on the other, Elly was shocked at the sharp contrast to the luxury of the hotel's lobby. There was business papers everywhere—in boxes on the floor, scattered on the desks and in heaps atop the filing cabinets.

A large woman with snow-white hair occupied the isolated desk, which sported a miniature teddy bear holding a sign that read, "Grin and bear it." Smiling, she gave Elly a wink of support, and Elly flashed a quick smile. To the right, on the other side of the cabinets, a pretty dark-haired woman with glasses sat at the only tidy desk. She appeared to be completely engrossed in neat little stacks of invoices, oblivious to everything around her. She was, in fact, sneaking furtive glances at Elly above the rim of her glasses.

When they reached Mr. Stewart's door, the receptionist raised her eyebrows at Elly and gave three quick raps, obviously implying he would recognize her signal. Hearing his muffled, "Come in," she opened the door for Elly with a smug look of satisfaction.

Byron Stewart immediately stood up. More than six feet tall, he towered above Elly as his twinkling eyes swept over her. His angular face had authority etched into every crevice, but his smile was warm. "Well, well, could it be the illustrious Mrs. Thomas adorning my office this morning?" He sounded as if he were quoting Shakespeare.

"Yes, sir, 'tis the one and only Mrs. Thomas, your new office manager for thee to interview," replied Elly in kind. She held his gaze and flashed her "melt an iceberg" smile as she extended her hand. He chuckled at her brashness and shook it.

The receptionist had left the door slightly ajar and didn't care that both Mr. Stewart and Elly could hear her. "Can you believe it?" she snickered to her coworkers. "The la-de-da redhead told Stewart she's the new office manager for Sunshine. Who in Sam's hell does she think she is—God's gift to office managers?" The responding laughter was shrill.

Silence hovered between Elly and Mr. Stewart until he finally said, flushing slightly, "Pay no attention to them. Please, sit down." He spoke crisply, with that distinct English rhythm she'd always admired. He gestured to a chair diagonally across from his desk and nervously shuffled papers.

She wasn't at all what he had anticipated. He was expecting someone older. She was far too attractive. *Blimey, those eyes are the biggest I've ever seen!* He raised himself in his chair, squared his shoulders and began, "This laundry is part of a chain owned by Summergrove Convention Center, Inc. It services all the bed and table linen needs of this center, as well as the uniforms for the bellhops, chefs and chambermaids. We also contract to clean cooks' apparel and mats—and we sell other products for restaurants and businesses along the California coastline."

He explained the salary and benefits offered, and then met Elly's eyes squarely. "See this? You have a lot of competition," he said, his tone now curt, pointing to a sheaf of applications six inches high. "This town is in a recession. Hundreds are looking for employment, many of them chartered accountants. Why should I hire you?"

"I've heard many comments about this company and how well it's run," Elly replied, avoiding his question in favor of a compliment to start. "And I understand you've had a run of bad luck with the management of your office," she continued, quietly adding, "when you had a man in this position. Perhaps it's time for a change of gender."

Mr. Stewart was a bit flustered at her directness and thought, *The lady has done her homework!* "That's true," he conceded. "We've had difficulty keeping office managers. They come and they go. And right now, I'm afraid, they're a dime a dozen! Tell me, what is your philosophy for a well-run office?"

"I firmly believe that if employees feel appreciated and are happy, the job gets done automatically," she replied. She surprised herself with her own wisdom.

He nodded sagely, "Jolly good! But how do you go about making the employees happy? Put more shillings in their pockets!"

She continued in her soft tone, "I believe true happiness on the job ultimately comes from pride in one's work. A manager must always show respect to the employee. He must always exhibit fairness and show appreciation. These are the intangibles that cannot be put in a paycheck."

Mr. Stewart smiled. "I agree with you, but it isn't always easy when dealing with a union agreement—grievances constantly being slapped on one's desk. Now, I see you have a lot of experience collecting outstanding accounts. What kind of philosophy do you have for that?"

"I believe the rules of the game should be established at the onset," she replied. "The customer should be informed of the terms at the time of his engagement. And he should be contacted immediately if he breaks these terms. A simple collection control system, where one can keep track of all customers, should be in place."

"That's absolutely correct." Mr. Stewart formed a steeple with his index fingers as he pursed his lips in deep contemplation. "I see from your application you've done some hiring, too. But tell me, have you ever fired anyone?"

"No, I haven't. I do realize that, today, it is difficult to legally fire someone," she stated. "One needs to build a file with a well-documented history of problems the employee has caused. If it is for the betterment of the company and a firing is necessary, I'd have no choice in the matter."

"Hmmm," was all he uttered as he reached across his desk and picked up the thick stack of applications and riffled through them. He pursed his lips again. Elly sat unmoving, hoping he had been impressed and was seriously considering her for the position. Finally, he broke the silence and said, "As I mentioned earlier, you have a lot of competition. I'll have to think this over." Fanning the stack of applications with his long fingers again, he blew some papers off his desk and bent to retrieve them.

Taking this as her cue the interview was over, Elly stood up and said softly, "Thank you very much."

After she closed the door behind her, he tossed the applications into his wastebasket, all except hers. He thought of the other candidates he'd interviewed, who all had emphasized their skills at preparing a budget. First and foremost, he required harmony in his office, and if he were to be successful in keeping a team together, the budget had to be his concern—his alone.

The receptionist pretended to be startled when Elly approached her and said, "Kindly give this to Mr. Stewart with tomorrow morning's mail," handing her a small, white envelope.

"I think I can manage that," she replied, snatching it from Elly's hand. After Elly left, the receptionist held the envelope up for the others to see and said, "I wonder what this is. La-de-da wants me to give it to Mr. Stewart."

"Is it sealed?" the plump woman asked.

"No, the flap is only tucked in."

"Go ahead! Open it! No one will know." The plump woman giggled shrilly as she moved around the file cabinets to the reception area.

"I intend to. Don't get your big ass in a knot," retorted the receptionist. She nimbly opened the envelope and slipped the white card out. The front of the glossy card simply read, "Thank you" in black italic letters. The blank interior held a note in fine penmanship.

Dear Mr. Stewart,

Thank you for taking the time from your busy schedule to interview me.

Elly Thomas

As soon as she'd finished reading it, she heard Stewart's footsteps coming from his office and swiftly slipped the card back into its envelope. Just as quickly, the plump woman blurted, "Byron, Janet has something to give you." He read the note and tucked it into his shirt pocket with a smile of satisfaction.

The next morning when Elly answered the phone, there was no hello, just the question, "When can you start?"

"Oh, it's Mr. Stewart!" she exclaimed, not immediately recognizing the voice. "I'll need to speak with my bosses, first. They're finishing a posting job and aren't expected back until four o'clock. I'm sure we can arrange a start date. Is it alright if I contact you first thing in the morning?"

"Phone me by ten o'clock. Oh, and one more thing, please keep it confidential for now. I plan to post a memo on the bulletin board. I don't want the employees to hear about it ahead of time."

"A secret it is!"

"Jolly good!"

As she hung up, her heart began thumping wildly. "I got it! Thank God!" she whispered, but her joy quickly turned to trepidation. *Now I have to tell the bosses. And Monday is just around the corner. I wonder what they'll say. Ah, shoot, they had no compunction about robbing my paycheck!"*

The day seemed endless, but at long last Pete and Easton returned. Elly knocked on the office door. "Can I talk to you both for a moment?" Her stomach felt queasy.

"Come right in," Easton replied, settling back in his chair.

"Business has really dried up here, hasn't it?" Elly began. Easton replied, "That's an understatement!"

"I'm wondering how long my position here will last. We barely make payroll now."

A look of relief washed over Easton's face. It was a sensitive subject that needed broaching. "We can't guarantee anything in these conditions—maybe three months and then again maybe just six weeks."

Pete joined in, with his thumbs hooked into the money belt, "Yeah, maybe six weeks. And maybe we'll be forced to take, I mean reduce, your paycheck again." He sounded almost gleeful. Easton, embarrassed, coughed and shifted in his chair.

"I'll save you the trouble." Elly spoke softly. "I've been offered a manager's job at the convention center and I've agreed to start Monday."

"You're jumping ship?" Pete snapped, as though it were the last thing he expected. just like that?"

"I have no choice, Pete," she replied. "It's imperative I help provide for my family. Our twins are heading off to university and medical school—that's an expensive proposition. If anyone can understand that, it's you."

Pete turned and walked out.

"Don't pay any attention to him," said Easton apologetically. "He'd do likewise if he were in your position."

"Thanks, Jerry," Elly replied, glad the altercation was over and anxious to go home and tell Vincent about her most interesting day.

"I would like you to phone everyone who owes us money before the end of the week and give me a final report on Friday morning," Easton said.

"I'll get right on it in the morning." As she was leaving, she turned and simply said, "Thanks, Jerry." He smiled and nodded.

Vincent was waiting for her when she arrived home that day, pretending to read the paper. But before she could close the door, he asked, "Well, how'd it go?'

"How'd what go?" she replied, making big eyes.

"Don't hand me any of that guff, woman. How'd it go?"

"Oooh, you mean the job interview," she cooed. "There were over a hundred applicants and some were chartered accountants—that's pretty stiff competition." He was silent for a moment as he tried to form the proper consolatory response, his serious expression making her laugh. "But he selected me!" She laughed again, as he jumped up and swung her around.

"Isn't that something, Vincent? There's a recession all over, and I land a new position just like that! By the way, Mr. Stewart asked that it be kept confidential, something about posting it on the bulletin board. I told you because I know if anyone can be trusted, it's you—being cleared for top secret in the military and all," she quipped.

Before Elly knew it, Friday arrived. She'd spent every conceivable moment that week phoning the clients on the accounts receivable list, missing no one. When she handed Easton the accounting report and new promise of substantial cash, he thanked her profusely for her efforts and continued, "We would like to take you to a farewell lunch today at noon."

At the lunch, Elly was delighted to see that Easton had invited Rachel, whom she hadn't seen in several months. She had brought along her baby daughter with hair the color of corn flax, whose incessant cooing drew laughter from everyone. "Here is a small token for our sincere appreciation for all your hard work," said Easton. "We've especially appreciated the extra work you've so graciously done, Elly." Looking at the lovely silver steins Easton presented, Elly was overcome with melancholy, remembering her enthusiasm when Lamoure had hired her all those years earlier and how the terrible incident with Simcoe and then the boss's passing had destroyed the spirit of the office so quickly.

But her melancholy was lifted when she gazed at Rachel's baby girl. She represented "new life." Now, Elly, too, would be starting a new life. No doubt, from her first impressions of the office staff, it held many challenges, but she knew she could rise to the occasion.

She was infinitely stronger and worldlier now, no longer needing to lean on Vincent. Her experiences with Lamoure Land Development had given her all the fortitude the future could ever demand, of that she was positive. *All of my yesterdays have created the woman I am today. And this day will be added to the mix, making me who I'll be tomorrow. Life is evolving.* With that thought, her excitement began to grow and she could hardly wait for Monday morning to arrive.

9

Dirty Laundry

Dark clouds hanging in the Summerville sky finally broke loose, giving the little California town the deluge of the decade. But in less than a week, the sun broke through and pulled blossoms and leaves from the stark branches. And the sun was shining for Elly today, the first day of her new job. She had ignored a tall, dark man wearing sunglasses who insisted on directing her into a parking place, casting a blind eye to his gesturing as she backed neatly into a spot. She was relieved to see him walking away when she opened the car door.

She had complemented her slim figure with a fitted, black gabardine suit, a red silk blouse and red suede pumps adding the finishing touch. She had read that black and red were colors of power and supposed it couldn't hurt to give it a try. She'd won the hair battle with Vincent, and now it was shorter and swept away from her face. She wanted to look her absolute best, and she did.

She walked swiftly across the parking lot and again encountered Sammy, the smoky vendor, adeptly flipping large smoked sausages from one plump side to the other in preparation for the early shift. "Good morning, Sammy," she said, beaming. "Sausages sure smell good this morning."

G'day ma'am, it looks like we finally have some sunshine," he said, squinting from the smoke.

"Yes, I'd say spring has arrived! Wouldn't you?" she replied joyfully. "I hope you're flooded with customers today, Sammy," she called over her shoulder.

His eyes followed her until she disappeared around the corner, red curls bouncing in the sunlight. He was elated.

At the front door, Elly inadvertently stepped in a puddle, her right shoe immediately saturated. "Oh, damn, nothing like wrecking my image!" she mumbled, shaking the water out. And there was no way to muffle the sucking sound as she walked across the lobby and down the long hallway toward Mr. Stewart's door—nor could she silence the giggling staff as they watched their new office manager squishing across the room on her first day of work. But she could ignore their sniggers.

Mr. Stewart's open door indicated he was waiting for her. Coming around to the front of his desk, he shook her hand and said, "Good morning, Elly. Welcome aboard! A little accident with a puddle, I see. Unfortunate bit of luck this morning—hope it wasn't cold! I've requested the engineering blokes to repair those gaps when time avails."

Elly flashed a dimpled smile. "Nothing I can't survive, Mr. Stewart. It'll dry."

"By the way, Elly, please feel free to call me Byron—all the other managers do. But the general staff is a different story—I've insisted they address me as Mr. Stewart. I'm a little old-fashioned in that regard—British background, you understand." He glanced at his watch. "I believe the other managers are out visiting customers, so I'll take you straightaway on a tour of the plant."

Passing through the main office on their way to the plant, he approached the dark-haired lady at the tidy desk. "This is

Rita, your computer operator. She's in charge of the computerized accounts—that is to say, all data entering and output of invoices." Rita looked up at Elly with sparkling brown eyes and nodded warmly.

Then Mr. Stewart made his way over to the large, white-haired woman seated next to the file cabinet. "And this is Melody. She looks after payroll and bank deposits." Melody giggled a hello while trying to straighten her rumpled t-shirt. A jumble of paperwork was scattered on her desk.

Finally, Mr. Stewart headed across the room toward the door. "And this young lady is Suzie Wing, our receptionist." Suzie averted her eyes, and her greeting was barely audible Elly smiled, nodding to each one in turn as she repeated their names. "Very nice to meet all of you," she said in an authoritative voice as she followed Stewart out of the room.

Behind her back, Suzie the receptionist turned to her coworkers and poked her finger into her open mouth in a gagging gesture. Melody giggled nervously, but Rita scolded, "Grow up, Suzie!"

Elly followed Mr. Stewart down the hallway toward the plant, doubling her pace to match his long strides. The large room they entered was bustling with activity. To the immediate right, a pressing machine expelled curls of steam from its sides. Elly watched in amazement for a few moments as an elderly woman brought the large padded cover down hard on the entire left side of a shirt, leaving it absolutely wrinkle-free in one step.

"As you can see, that's the ironer. We have different pressing machines downstairs," Mr. Stewart noted. "And over there to the right is where all the counting in is done. We count in the dirty garments for the contract jobs to determine the amount to invoice. All payments go into the Sunshine Linen account, and once a month we transfer a portion to Summergrove Convention Center's general account."

"I see," Elly replied, wondering if there was a cash flow problem here, as there had been at Lamoure Land Development.

They walked toward the count-in station, Mr. Stewart purposely stopping about five feet away. In a few seconds, Elly realized why the stench was overwhelming! The count-in clerk, an elderly woman with filthy hands, dyed black hair and a hanging wart on the side of her nose, scrutinized Elly brazenly then quickly switched her gaze to the man in charge. "Morn'n, Mr. Stewart."

He barely nodded before turning to Elly and continuing, "Those laundry bags running on the track overhead have been hoisted off the truck that unloads at the side door." Elly nodded, thinking they looked like sides of beef hanging in cold storage. "Ninety percent of our revenue is derived from this convention center. The remaining ten percent comes from the mills, garages and Summergrove's main restaurants. We do some business with the retirement homes, and every uniformed person on the local ferry wears our textile. We also sell allied products, like bathroom supplies and rubber mats, to a multitude of businesses all up and down the coast, large and small."

He gestured to the count-in table. "When the clerk pulls the cord, the bag dumps its dirty load on the table. If it's from a restaurant, old food and cigarette butts often spill out along with the table linens. When it's from a garage or mill, the uniforms smell like oil and often have tools left in the pockets. Those are turned in to the office, and the customer is called. The count-in clerk is critical to the accounting function. She counts the lot—that is, all the different rental items—and lists them on a packing slip that she then passes to Rita, who enters these totals into the computer and then prints the invoice for the next delivery."

"Where do the items go after she's counted them?"

"As the clerk is counting them, she tosses them into their designated shoots near her table. They land in a box by the washing machines in the basement, ready to be thrown into washers, load by load."

The clerk's blackened hands moved rapidly as she counted the garments. The foul smell stung Elly's nostrils, and she wondered how anyone could do such a filthy job eight hours a day, five days a week. She was nauseated after just a few minutes and from a distance!

Mr. Stewart pointed toward a large, open doorway. "That is the storeroom. We keep a large, valuable inventory of new items to replace the ones that wear out. The customer signs a contract to rent our product, and we promise to keep it clean and in good condition. We replace only when we have to—otherwise, it is repaired."

Elly could see shelves laden with table linens in many different colors. She could also see cooks' apparel hanging on suspended rods and was amazed by the quantity. "I had no idea. I thought Sunshine Linen was merely a local laundry, washing individual clothing," she confessed.

"A lot of people think the same," he replied. "In fact, we are one of many large conglomerates along the Pacific Coast." As they continued to walk, he gestured to a young woman working diligently at a sewing machine. She wore a neck brace, and Elly wondered whether it was because she had whiplash or because the strenuous job demanded it. "She keeps the garments in excellent repair," Mr. Stewart noted. "I don't know what she's done to her neck."

He strode across the room to an aluminum box that had steam escaping from an opening at each end. "This is what we call the 'steam tunnel.' It removes wrinkles from the garments, route by route," he explained, pointing to a circuit of tracks, connected to a pulley, that ran through the steam tunnel.

Elly could see several long tracks of garments—bellhop suits, chef coats and chambermaid uniforms—converging and waiting their turn to pass through. The results were remarkable. "That must save an awful lot of ironing," she commented.

"Yes, that's the whole idea. We press only what's required because ironing is labor intensive—and labor cost is our biggest enemy. We try to save everywhere we can, in order to make yearly budget." Elly nodded, but the phrase "save everywhere we can" stuck in her mind. "Now, allow me to show you the basement," he continued.

Elly followed him down steep, curving wooden stairs that were so badly worn she feared falling. An expansive laundry operation lay within the bowels of the building. Large washing machines, extractors, pressing machines and dryers droned so loudly that he had to cup his hands around his mouth when he told Elly all these machines didn't come cheap. Her eyes swept over the large machines and rested on the name "Huebsch" stamped on the front of one. Although she'd not heard it before, she surmised it was manufactured in Germany.

The smell of bleach and fabric fiber was everywhere, coupled with a tinge of tar from the rubber-backed mats piled on the floor. Although pungent, the smell was a welcome reprieve from the count-in station. There were many workers here, feeding table linens through a large roller, folding bar towels from a wooden bin on rollers and wrapping folded linens in plastic for the route trucks. With the exception of a man feeding the washing machines, all were women of advancing age. Elly wondered again how they could do this kind of work eight hours a day, five days a week. And once again, she recalled her earlier life and the lack of fulfillment she felt doing mundane housework—especially the laundry.

They slowly made their way back up the stairs and into the office, the tour over. "I'll show you to your office," Mr. Stewart said. "It's right beside mine—so I can keep a watchful eye on you." He laughed and the angles of his face softened. The transformation remarkable.

"Or the other way around," she teased back gently, carefully testing his receptiveness to returned kidding, and was pleased when he chuckled loudly. Hearing this friendly repartee, Suzie and Melody rolled their eyes at one another.

Keeping an eye on me would be a fulltime job," he quipped. "Here're your keys—the largest one is for the front door. I've placed last week's journal and all-important chart of accounts on your desk for your perusal. You will also find an overview of my expectations of your position. I suggest you look everything over very carefully." His voice became stern, "In addition, the top desk drawer holds a booklet—the Union Contract. I want you to take it home and study it every spare moment you have. I insist you become as familiar with the contract as the back of your hand. I cannot stress that enough!" The ominous ring to his voice sounded like a warning.

Elly fiddled with the key momentarily but, after giving the knob a quick jerk, finally managed to open the door. She was astonished at the sight of her new "home away from home." Dust-covered cardboard file boxes dating as far back as twenty years were lined up against one wall stacked three high. A bottom box, exhausted from the weight, had buckled and released its contents through the grip holes. A small bookcase directly across the small room—under the one window, which was covered with a dingy curtain—was stuffed to capacity with dusty books, journals, copies of general ledger sheets, two empty Coke bottles, a roll of twine and two unused mouse traps. She shuddered at the thought of a mouse scuttling around her feet on the heavily stained carpet.

The only clean surface in the room was the top of the gray metal desk, which held last week's journal and several letter-size sheets stapled together that bore the title "Chart of Accounts." The desk drawer was crammed so full, she had to pry it open. Lying on top of the muddle was the union contract booklet, which she tucked into her purse and a scribbled note with "Elly's Duties" written at the top.

The duties included bank reconciliation, staffing, payroll and benefits, overseeing the total office accounting function and so on, but it was the final duty, underlined in red that Elly found surprising: protector of corporate funds. It sounded so officious, almost a warning. She recalled seeing a safe bolted to the floor in the main office and made a mental note to make certain it was locked at all times—and she couldn't help thinking of Simcoe.

Oh, where to start? Elly asked herself, looking around the dreadful office. *Before I can do any work at all, I must clean!* Returning from the washroom with a supply of wet paper towels, she began to wipe things down. When Stewart walked past her open door, he paused and, looking sheepish, said, "My apologies for the mess in your office. The janitor has been sick, and the engineers are only doing what's absolutely necessary. I must always consider labor costs, you know."

"No problem," Elly replied. "It'll only take me a minute."

Finally able to sit down at her desk in the dilapidated high-back chair with its stained cushion, she looked out into the main office at her staff. She knew becoming acquainted with them would take time, but she wanted to get the process started. With this thought in mind, she called a meeting in her office. "I appreciate you coming in, ladies. Please have a chair. I'd like to take just a few moments for us to become acquainted. My name is Elly Thomas—you can call me Elly. I'd be pleased if each of you would tell me something about yourselves, your history with Sunshine Linen, job duties and so on." She smiled infectiously, while looking at each in turn, checking for signs of acceptance. "Rita, you have the honor of being first."

"My name is Rita Skarvinsky. I'm married and have two beautiful daughters. I have been with the company since the age of seventeen—that's twenty-one years, altogether—and I haven't missed a day's work. I do the data entry—actually, all the important computer work." Her brooding brown eyes shone with fierce pride behind her glasses.

"You have a very important job, Rita. There's no question about that. I know you must be very busy, indeed," Elly said with sincerity.

"You've got that right, ma'am!" Rita replied and nudged Melody that it was her turn to speak.

"My name is Melody Uppler and I have three wonderful sons." The large woman giggled and added, "I recently divorced a lousy husband." Then she giggled again in a higher pitch. "I've been working here with Sunshine Linen as accounts receivable specialist for the past ten years. I guess that's half as long as Rita." She giggled again and shifted her weight in her chair, while keeping an unwavering eye on Elly.

"Not quite," corrected Rita.

"Oh, yes, I almost forgot. I balance the morning cash, enter the payments into the accounts and process payroll. I also answer the phone when Suzie's away from her desk."

"Thanks, Melody, you must have a full plate." Filled with regret for applying the term "full plate" to an overweight woman, Elly diverted her attention to Suzie, who was shifting in her chair, forming and reforming her words on her lips. Elly could see she was trying to decide whether she would speak.

Finally, with chin thrust forward, she blurted, "I'm Suzie Wing, and I ain't typing letters for no one—especially ain't doing it for the office manager."

"Really?" Elly replied, raising her brows and widening her eyes, a tactic that worked with her sons. She was glad to see Suzie flinch; it was slight, but a flinch nonetheless. Elly stood up, indicating the interview was over, and said, "If at any time any of you feel the need to talk to me about anything at all, please don't hesitate. My door is always open. Thanks again for coming in."

Elly was bothered by the crust of Suzie's words. Once again, she was seeing rivalry in the workplace, albeit from a different perspective. Perhaps this time, she'd be in a position to put a stop to it. She wondered what had put such a chip on Suzie's shoulder, and what it might take to win her over. Just as she was beginning to feel overwhelmed, she remembered Vincent's words when she had started with Lamoure, *if you really want to succeed in this, for heaven's sake, woman, give yourself some time!"* She drew comfort from the memory, recalling how those words had inspired her to continue on and eventually succeed.

A moment later, Suzie entered Elly's office and plopped a gigantic bundle of mail in the middle of her desk. It was the biggest stack of assorted envelopes she'd ever seen. She was fingering through the heap, thinking it would take at least an hour to open it all, when the phone rang. It was the post office three blocks away, saying a small parcel had arrived for pick up. She glanced toward Suzie's vacant desk and, guessing she was in the bathroom, scribbled a note asking her to fetch the parcel.

Later in the day, Elly was engrossed in the age listing and planning her collection strategy, when an irate woman burst into her office. She banged her fist on Elly's desk and screamed, "Dat's your job! Dat's your job!"

Elly vaguely remembered seeing her in the basement when Mr. Stewart gave her the tour but had no idea what she was shouting about. "Settle down," she ordered. "What's this job you say is mine?" The woman's ranting continued, drowning out Elly's voice. Finally she ran out of breath, and Elly spoke slowly and deliberately, although her heart was pounding. "If you have anything to say to me, you make an appointment. Don't ever barge into my office again!"

The woman stomped out and went immediately to Suzie's desk, whispering something to her before going back into the plant. Although Suzie's back was facing her, Elly could see her giggling and realized what the woman had been shouting about. Suzie simply did not want to pick up the parcel—the screaming woman was the shop steward. And Suzie had thoroughly enjoyed the ruckus. The shouting had brought Mr. Stewart onto the scene. Standing next to her doorway, he thought, *what a firecracker this new manager is!*

That evening, when she told Vincent about the incident, much to her amazement, he replied, "You handled it perfectly, Elly. I'm so proud of you!"

The next morning, Elly summoned Suzie to her office. She looked directly at Suzie for a few minutes with large, unwavering eyes, before saying, "When I assumed this position and we had our first meeting yesterday, I told you and the other staff that if you ever needed to talk to me, my door would always be open. Why didn't you tell me you were uncomfortable picking up the package yesterday?"

"I ... I didn't think you'd listen to me."

"Do you honestly think you were being fair?

"Well, no ... but ..."

"You're a bright girl, Suzie. I'm certain you can understand the importance of communication and fair play. In future, if anything—and I mean anything—is bothering you, promise me you will come into my office to discuss it." Elly flashed her "melt an iceberg" smile.

"Yes, ma'am," replied Suzie, her tone more sarcastic than courteous, and walked heavy-footed back to her desk. She would have felt better if Elly had scolded her. Her pleasantness, for some strange reason, left Suzie deflated. The blush on her face was exaggerated by her fair skin and broadcast to her co-workers that she'd been reprimanded.

Over the following weeks, Elly learned the rudiments of her new position, albeit in fractured pieces. Often she'd arrive to work early to finish paperwork. With paper deadlines met, she then had time to contemplate her staff working out front. Her field of vision also included the main entrance, where she could see patrons coming in. Although they were strangers now, she knew that would change. Her early arrivals also brought pleasant encounters with Sammy, whose endearing ways always provided a happy start to her day.

10

Labor Problems

Suzie had settled down after her gentle reprimand, but now Rita was causing concern. She had become withdrawn and developed deep circles under her eyes. *Before the day is through, I must have a talk with her,* Elly thought. She had barely concluded the thought when Eric Joyble, public relations officer for Sunshine Linen, appeared in her doorway.

This was their first one-on-one encounter, his frequent absences from the office preventing an earlier meeting. He stood rigidly in dark clothing, his carefully combed blond hair competing for shine with the tip of his aquiline nose. His sober face and officious manner indicated he wasn't paying her "a welcome to the company" visit.

There was something vaguely familiar about his cavalier manner, but she couldn't quite put her finger on it. "What can I do for you?" she asked, leveling her gaze to meet his and forcing a bright smile.

"Why didn't you pay me my bonus?" he asked accusingly, holding his paycheck up. Elly was baffled, and before she could reply, he continued, "My paycheck was never shorted when a man held your position." His steely-blue eyes bore through her, and although his protruding teeth caused a slight lisp, it did not stop his words from hitting home.

"What bonus?"

"On the second pay period of each month, I receive a bonus on the results of my department. I sure don't appreciate being gypped." He finished the sentence with his teeth clenched, shifting from one leg to the other.

"I'm sorry it's happened," Elly said, purposely maintaining a soft timbre in her voice. "I'll investigate right away and get back to you."

"It's imperative you tell me exactly what you're going to do about it … today," he replied, then turned on his heel and strode away. As she watched him leave, she remembered where she'd seen him. He was the man who tried to direct her into the parking space when she'd come for her interview. *Was he miffed because I ignored him that day?*

Entering Mr. Stewart's office, Elly asked soberly, "Eric Joyble has asked for his bonus. Is that something I should know about?"

"Oh, I'm so sorry," Mr. Stewart said, tapping his forehead in the "clueless me" gesture. "I should have given you his bonus schedule when you started." He reached into a file in the bottom drawer of his desk, quickly withdrew a sheet of paper and handed it to Elly. "Tell him, if he really needs the money now, we can cut a local check, or we can put it on his next pay, whatever he prefers." Elly nodded but wondered why he was smiling so ruefully.

Joyble's office was as tidy as a military bed top, not a single business paper on his desk. He sat rigidly in his desk chair, a nail clipper in his hand, and pretended not to notice Elly's approach.

"I can cut you a local check for your bonus immediately, if you like," Elly told him.

"Why on God's green acre would I want you to do that? I can wait until next payday," he replied, without looking up. He obviously was just trying to make things difficult for her.

An inner voice warned her to suppress the retorts that sprang to mind. "Alright," she replied, instead, "it's your call.

Returning to her desk, she decided to calculate his bonus anyway and put the paperwork in his file—heaven forbid she should miss it twice. When the calculation was complete, she was astounded to see it was a mere six dollars. Checking previous records, she found it had never been over ten. Offended by his pettiness, she realized that holding a position on the management team of Sunshine, a position traditionally held by a man, wasn't going to be a cakewalk. But she also knew acceptance was something time would fix and effort would earn.

She also realized that if she wanted to get her daily tasks done, she would have to either close her door or come in on Saturdays. People were constantly in and out of her office, dropping off receipts or bills of lading in the inbox on her desk or questioning something or other. *If I close the door, I cannot see what's happening in the main office. Better to put the inbox on the wall next to the doorway.* She rang for the house engineer to do the task.

Later in the day, Elly was immersed in the reconciliation of the first bank statement when she heard a light knock on her door. She didn't look up immediately, but when she did, she saw Rita standing there, twisting a tissue with both hands. "Can I talk to you?" she mumbled beneath her breath. "It's private."

"Of course, Rita, come in. Shut the door and have a seat."

Rita sat down and struggled to find her voice. "I need to have some time off, "she finally blurted. Then she buried her face in her hands and started to sob.

In a flash, Elly was around her desk and at her side. She took Rita's glasses off just before they fell and offered her a Kleenex. She placed her arm around her shoulders and gently squeezed. "Of course, you can have time off if you need it."

"My mother is dying! I need to look after her—she doesn't have anyone else. I've been going there three times a day, all the way to the other side of town—before work, at lunch and after work. I feel so sorry for her—she's suffering so much! And I'm so exhausted!" She blew her nose and continued, "As soon as I get time off, I'll be able to stay with her all day. The doctor says she's got … she's got just … only a few days."

Elly was overcome with compassion. *So that's why she's been so sullen and passive—she's been grieving, poor lady.* "I'm so sorry about your mother, Rita. We'll just have to find a replacement for you. I'll have to post a two-day notice for a possible replacement from within the plant workers first. But in the meantime, you can take either the afternoons or mornings off. I know you realize the importance of punching in the soil tickets and generating the invoices for the drivers' daily loads."

"Yes, I do, but … but there's no employee in the plant who can handle my job," Rita stammered.

"I don't think there is, either. But according to the union contract, it's imperative I post it. In the meantime, I think I know someone who'll be able to do the basics of your job while you're away. You'll have to give her some crash training so she can produce the soil tickets. All in all, in about three days you should be free to go."

"Thanks, Elly," Rita murmured. "Please don't tell Melody or Suzie until after I'm gone. They're just going to ask me a bunch of questions I don't feel like answering."

"Of course not, we'll keep it a secret. When your replacement comes in, I'll tell them you needed some time off. They don't need to know anything else about your circumstance until *you're* ready to tell them," Elly replied, making a mental note to cross-train the office staff as soon as possible for this very type of emergency. Visible relief washed over Rita's face as she left Elly's office and went into the computer room.

Elly's thoughts quickly turned to Debra Black, a neighbor she'd recently met who had expressed a desire to work in an office. "Part time to start would do me just nicely," she'd declared. On subsequent encounters on the street, she'd expressed the desire again and told Elly she'd recently completed a computer course after her husband purchased one for their home. "I simply don't understand why so many people are mystified by it," she said. "It's just a silly old machine!"

When Debra answered her door early that evening, she was surprised to find Elly standing on her front step. "Would you like a temporary job?" Elly asked, getting right to the point of the visit.

"Sure! Oh, my goodness! Really? Come on in."

"Sorry, I can't. I have something in the oven and have only a minute. Can you come to Sunshine tomorrow morning? I'll explain it to you then."

"What time?" asked Debra flustered with excitement.

"Nine in the morning would be great. Can you make it?"

"You betcha," replied Debra. "Nine it is. I'll be there with bells on!"

"See you tomorrow, then," replied Elly, smiling. As she hurried back to her house, a nagging thought made her wonder if it was a good idea to hire a neighbor. She quickly dismissed her worry. *Why not? If it isn't my neighbor, it'll be someone else's.*

At nine o'clock sharp Debra walked into Elly's office. Suzie glared at her back as she entered. "Good morning," said Elly cheerfully. "Great you're right on time. I hate it when people are late. Come in and sit down. And please shut the door so we have privacy while we go over a few things." Debra sat down, her eyes wide with anticipation. "The job that's coming up is for a computer operator. It's a temporary position, but if it works out, you could have a job most of the summer, replacing staff as they take their annual vacations. It's a union position, so I have to post it first for three days. I placed it on the bulletin board yesterday. So by next Monday, the job is yours if no one from within applies, which I highly doubt. The hours are eight to four thirty." "Wonderful!" Debra exclaimed. "I've been looking around for some time but just haven't been able to find anything. Everyone these days wants someone with a whole lot of experience."

"The beauty of this job is that we will teach you the basics. You'll learn as you go. At first, you'll be a little slow, but after a while you'll find a comfortable speed. It's straight data entering and printing of the invoices. It's a very important job, Debra—the customers' deliveries depend entirely upon the computer operator generating the packing slips. It's the very beginning of the accounting and production wheel of this business."

"Sounds great, I like to do important work. I'll be here on Monday with bells on!"

Elly stood and rubbed her hands together, happy to have solved the first major problem of her new position. "Great! I'll see you Monday morning, then. Kindly close the door on your way out." She was relieved Debra wanted the job. The computer operator's position was critical. If it stopped, everything stopped. No doubt an ad in the local paper would, in this time of recession, draw a multitude of applications, but she did not have time to interview and screen many—hiring someone quickly was paramount.

"I know how hard these next few days will be for you, Rita," Elly said, giving her a hug. "I'll be thinking of you." Heartfelt sincerity showed in her eyes.

"Thanks, Elly. I'll phone you just as soon as I can when … when … it happens."

Elly saw Rita's chin quiver before she turned and walked slowly out the door, the world on her shoulders, and couldn't help drawing parallels between Lamoure Land Development and Sunshine Linen.

The first week after Rita's departure passed smoothly. Debra learned quickly and performed the job with remarkable efficiency. However, Suzie spent an inordinate amount of time whispering to Debra and assuming the role of trainer. Elly could see they had become very friendly, indeed, and was uncomfortable about it. It was a tossup between talking to Suzie about it and perhaps creating a worse situation, or waiting to see if Debra would stop it herself. Melody, on the other hand, had become very attentive to her job since the new employee had been added to the mix.

The Monday morning of Debra's second week, Mr. Stewart walked past Elly's doorway and made an exaggerated gesture toward his watch. Elly was perplexed until she saw that Debra's desk was empty—and it was quarter after eight. All Sunshine Linen employees, according to their union contract, clocked in at eight o'clock sharp. Elly was embarrassed that Stewart noticed Debra's absence before she had. "Has Debra called in?" she asked.

Suzie swung around in her chair, grinning. "Nope."

Finally, at eight twenty-five, a smiling Debra bounced in and nonchalantly took her place at her desk. Elly waited a few moments to see if she would come explain her tardiness, but she obviously had no intention of doing so. Elly phoned her and asked her to come into her office. "No doubt you are aware, Debra, work here commences at 8:00 A.M. for everyone. Your tardiness has held up the packing slips. The drivers are waiting for them in the lunchroom. Production has come to a virtual standstill! Why were you late? Moreover, why didn't you telephone?" Elly's eyes had darkened to emerald as they bore into Debra's.

Debra shifted uncomfortably from one foot to the other. "Oh, I'm only twenty minutes late—that's nothing. The power was off, and my alarm clock didn't ring."

"You should have phoned me," Elly scolded.

"How could I phone you when I was sleeping?" Debra retorted.

"Look," said Elly, "I have a spare windup alarm clock at home. I'll bring it in tomorrow, so you won't have to be dependent on electricity."

"If you wish," Debra said and marched back to her desk. Seconds later, Suzie was at her side, whispering and giggling.

The following morning, Elly positioned the alarm clock in the middle of Debra's desk. Two days passed and Debra was late again. At eight thirty, she strolled through the front door, bypassed the time clock and marched directly into Elly's office with heavy footsteps. "I forgot to wind the damn thing," she blurted before Elly could collect her thoughts.

"You have been late twice this week. If it happens again, I'll have no choice but to document it, Debra," Elly admonished.

Debra could see Elly was angry, but she wasn't in the mood for a reprimand. She simply turned around and proceeded to her desk. Suzie immediately joined her, papers in hand in the pretense of business. Soon they were both giggling. "What a mean bag she is!" Debra declared.

"Tell me about it!" Suzie responded.

Stunned, Elly sat there for a few minutes, contemplating the situation. She needed the girl to do the job she was hired to do. She also needed her to arrive on time, especially before other union members complained. She really felt like giving Debra her walking papers. Unfortunately, she had no replacement, so she would have to struggle on. She also knew there was a procedure to follow for when the time came. She withdrew a notebook from her desk and made note of the incidences of tardiness for future reference. Somehow, the action provided some solace.

The numerous unemployed union people in Summergrove had planned a march for that day to protest layoffs at the local mill. The event was called Marching for Solidarity. They planned to congregate at the courthouse at noon and march along certain streets for the rest of the afternoon. When Suzie and Debra were out for their coffee break, Melody came into Elly's office and said, "There's something very important you need to know, Elly. Suzie and Debra are going to let their jobs go to hell and march this afternoon. They're going to walk off their jobs, right out the door without your permission, and march. Can you believe they would do such a thing?"

"Honestly, I can. Thanks for telling me, Melody. I really appreciate it. You've done the right thing."

Elly kept a close vigil. When the girls went into the hallway in preparation to leave, she was hot on their trail. "Hold it right there!" she commanded, hands on her hips and eyes blazing. "If you ladies think you're marching for solidarity today, you'd better think again. If you walk away from your jobs, you both will be suspended immediately … without pay!" Shocked by her stern words, they returned to their desks somberly.

The next morning, Debra's desk was vacant well past starting time. When she did arrive, she marched directly into Elly's office and declared loudly that she was late because she was constipated and couldn't leave the bathroom. Giggles from the others resounded throughout the office. Elly just shook her head. "I've heard many excuses in my day, but this is a classic. Go to your desk, Debra, and do your job. The trucks are waiting for their loads." After Debra left, she reached into her desk for the secret notebook and noted the date, writing, "constipated" beside it

The entire situation was wearing on Elly, so much so that she'd developed a nagging pain in the bottom of her stomach. She rubbed her hands over her face in exasperation. *I'll sure be happy when Rita returns.* No sooner had the thought crossed her mind than the phone rang, and it *was* Rita. "I buried my mom yesterday. It was horrible!" she cried. "I desperately need to return to the office. I'm going crazy here at home, thinking about everything. Is it possible for me to return on Monday?"

"I'll be delighted to have you return! I've missed you terribly. You won't believe what's happened since you've been away," Elly exclaimed.

"Oh, thank goodness," Rita declared with a sigh of relief. "You can fill me in on Monday. See you then!"

At day's end, it was with a mixture of joy and regret that Elly handed Debra a letter that clearly stated she was not suitable to become the office back-up person due to her tardiness and that she was relieved of her duties herewith. Debra read it then threw her head back and laughed. "I'll let you in on a little secret. I wasn't planning on coming to work on Monday, anyway. My husband and I are moving to Los Angeles. How does that grab you, Mrs. Thomas?"

Elly didn't respond. There was nothing further she wished to say to this person. Instead, she walked quietly back to her office and reflected on the past two weeks and one girl's ungratefulness. A hand held out in friendship hadn't received even a smidgen of thanks. She was happy to be seeing the last of Debra and happy she was moving out of the neighborhood.

Elly's next task would be finding a summer holiday replacement person. She didn't expect to encounter a problem. The unemployment situation in Summergrove would provide her with many choices. And in the future, she would interview and check references—even if it meant doing it at home after dinner.

But a far more important lesson had been learned: if the office was to run efficiently, cross-training of staff was paramount. Each office employee should be able to float from one desk to the others. She placed this at the top of her list of things to accomplish, while grimacing from the sharp pain in her stomach.

11

Tragedy Averted

It wasn't until the middle of summer that Elly realized her office sat squarely above a large dryer in the basement; the heat was inescapable. The drone of the engine destroyed her tranquility, while her small fan scattered anything the paperweight hadn't nailed down. She tried opening the one window for a fresh breeze, until the traffic noise forced her to close it.

Despite the heat, harmony prevailed among the staff. However, Elly noticed a marked change in Mr. Stewart's demeanor. He usually made regular rounds of the plant, whistling melodiously—an indication to everyone nearby that he was taking notice—but lately, he'd become a recluse, remaining in his office with the door closed. It was clear to Elly he did not want to talk, but she knew there must be a disturbance of some magnitude in his life.

Yet, the bigger question concerning Elly was why she was feeling so poorly. She'd first noticed the pain in her lower abdomen while Rita was away. It kept coming and going, leaving her exhausted. At first, she had attributed it to the tension caused by Debra, but that was now a month ago.

As she walked slowly out to the parking lot at the end of a long, hot week, grateful for the weekend reprieve, she encountered Sammy once again. *He's working late,* she thought. "How's it going, Sammy? Are you having a dog gone good day?"

"You bet I am," he replied. "Best day ever! But I have some I already cooked left over. I'll have to throw them out, so I was wondering if you'd like to take them home for your guys."

"Why, Sammy, that's really good of you! I would love to have them," said Elly, remembering how Vince and the boys had devoured the last bunch she'd taken home. As she waited while he carefully packaged them for her, double-wrapping them in foil to keep them warm, another piercing pain flashed across her abdomen, held steady for a moment and then finally dissipated. *Yikes! What's wrong with me?* she wondered again.

Her question was answered when she got home. Vincent was waiting, his face ashen, his blue eyes tear-filled. His large hand trembled as he handed her the single-page letter that had arrived from the Summergrove Clinic. Elly read it and reread it. That night she couldn't eat dinner.

The next morning, she carefully backed her car into the vacant spot of the parking lot, just as she had when she'd come for her interview six months earlier. This time, there was something much more daunting ahead. She'd lain awake all night, worrying what the doctor would tell her—his letter had said only that it was an urgent matter. Now, after her early morning visit to his office, she knew.

She dreaded having to face Mr. Stewart with this bad news and ask for time off. He didn't answer her knock at first. Finally, she heard his muffled "come in" above the roar of the washing machines under his office floor.

"I need to speak with you ... about something important," Elly began, her heart racing.

He stared at her blankly, wide-eyed and brooding, his long fingers forming a church steeple, before finally answering, "Yes?"

"I've just visited my gynecologist, and he's given me some horrible news. I need to have emergency surgery … tomorrow."

"Surgery!" Mr. Stewart roared. "How long will you be gone?

I'm told recovery time is about six weeks. But I have a strong constitution, so I believe I can be back—at least, in the mornings—after three. And it's only the fourth of the month, so I'll be back in time to finish the daily journals and complete the month end. I can do the payroll calculations and mail them ahead to the head office. There shouldn't be too much inconvenience." She saw his eyebrows rise and heard his silence roar. Her face flushed. "It won't cost the company anything," she concluded.

"You knew this when I hired you, didn't you?" he barked accusingly.

Elly was shocked and cut to the quick by his lack of sympathy. "No, I didn't. Honestly, I only found out last night." The pain in her stomach was grinding and she began to feel faint.

"My wife is a nurse. I know about these things—they don't just suddenly happen overnight. I don't believe you for one moment. I'm cutting off your pay. And we'll see what happens when you get back—that's if you ever do. I've had so much bloody trouble with the other office managers, I really don't need any more from you now."

"Sorry," she murmured, for appeasement purposes only.

"Sorry—" he mocked, "that's merely a word."

Her heart was heavy and her eyes smarting as she turned to leave. The lump in her throat remained for the rest of the morning and throughout the early afternoon as she worked through the paperwork, paving the road for her time away. Finally confident she'd covered everything, she left the suffocating atmosphere of the office at 2:00 P.M. to pre-register at the hospital.

Once again, she encountered Sammy on the street, but today he didn't seem his usual perky self, either. Although it was difficult for Elly to present a cheerful front, she realized their repartee had become important to Sammy and greeted him jovially, "Good afternoon, Sammy. My goodness, you look as if you've lost your best friend!"

"All my customers have disappeared—haven't sold one smoky today, not a solitary one. I'm beginning to get a complex!" His frown made him look like Mr. Magoo.

"They haven't all disappeared, Sammy! You have a customer right here who's willing to take a half dozen off your hands immediately."

"Really six, ma'am?"

"Sure! I can heat them later for the three hungry guys at my house. They're really quite delicious, Sammy!"

"Gee, thanks, that's very benevolent of you. You know, I'd recognize you anywhere, but after all this time, I still don't know your name.

"It's Elly Thomas, short for Elspeth." She smiled broadly, despite the tormenting ache in her abdomen.

"Thanks, Elly, you just made my day! I've never finished a day empty-handed." In fact, she really had made his day—for that matter, his week. He'd been waiting for an encounter with her all week. When she'd walked away, Sammy took a little notepad out of his pocket and carefully entered her name. Beside it, he wrote, "The nicest person I know."

And Elly was thinking when she left that benevolent was rather a big word for this humble little man.

By noon the next day, her operation was over. Fortunately, the doctor had caught the cervical cancer just in the nick of time. When he ordered pap tests at six-month intervals, Elly didn't mind at all—her health must come first now. On her third day in the hospital, Rita came to visit, arms laden with gifts, including some salmon preserved in Mason jars. "It makes beautiful sandwiches," she said. "Everything is going smoothly at work—you don't have to worry about a thing. I've put all the correspondence marked 'confidential' on your desk and opened and distributed the rest.

"I'll sure be happy when you come back, though—the office is God awful boring without you. And guess what—Byron said the identical thing to me just this morning! He's been asking about you—every day, he asks about you. I told him you're just fine, as good as new, but he keeps asking, as though I'm hiding something. I think he's afraid you won't come back." The look in her eyes told Elly she understood the importance of those words, and it was precisely then that Elly began to consider Rita her true friend.

After Rita left, Elly heard laughter coming from the nursing station and instantly recognized it as Melody's. For the first time, she enjoyed hearing it—in fact, she found it endearing. All flushed and tussled, Melody swooped into the room with a potted, pink African violet in her hands and a big smile on her face.

"How lovely, Melody! My favorite color - pink!"

"I can't stay—I have a friend waiting in the car—I just wanted you to know we're missing you at the office." She giggled again before ducking out the door. Elly was delighted her staff had visited and wasn't surprised one had stayed away. She knew she could never bond with Suzie and it would be pointless to try.

When Elly returned home from the hospital, her parents came to visit, bringing a number of delicious casseroles for easy suppers. And it seemed Vincent's new mission was waiting on her hand and foot. He brought hot soup, tea and little store-bought cakes to her bedside. The twins, who'd come home from university at the news of her illness, also pampered her. They lay on either side of her, nestling close like puppy dogs. She felt cherished and knew their care had stronger healing powers than all the medicine in the world. Soon she was back on her feet and raring to go

When she returned to work, Mr. Stewart called her into his office immediately. "How are you feeling, Elly?" Not waiting for her response, he continued, "I must apologize for the way I treated you when you told me about your operation. Actually, I hadn't been too well myself, if that can be an excuse for poor behavior. You know, I've never been very big on compliments, but I have to admit, you've become very important to this office." His face flushed, he could barely meet her penetrating gaze. "I'm sorry," he whispered huskily, his tone sincere.

Today, he's saying he is sorry! What a turn of events! "Sorry?" she teased. "Sorry is merely a word."

He replied sheepishly, "I know you're quoting me, but can we forget it all, Elly? Can you forgive this old Brit for his transgression?"

Silence hung in the room for what seemed an eternity. At last, Elly spoke, dimpling a smile, "Transgression? What transgression?" Stewart quickly rose and extended his hand. Elly shook it with vigor, adding a little squeeze. She knew her quick forgiveness had forged a new relationship with him—one she would guard carefully.

As she turned to leave, Mr. Stewart added, "By the way, Elly, I've put a pay increase through for a Mrs. Thomas. The details are on your desk. Please ensure this happens next payday—the lady deserves it."

It took a few seconds for his words to sink in. "Thank you," she managed, eyes misty. When she returned to her desk and read his note, she was astounded. He'd increased her salary by a whopping 25 percent.

Over the next few days, Elly noticed a marked change in the atmosphere of the office. Since returning from her surgery, a day hadn't passed without both Rita and Melody demonstrating their loyalty in one way or another. She was delighted to have their support, grateful for the harmony it created in the office. She knew efficiency and harmony go hand in hand.

Seeing these new relationships forming, Suzie decided it was time she befriended the new office manager and also high time she enlightened her about a few things. With this thought in mind, she lightly rapped on the doorframe of Elly's office. "Can I talk to you for a few moments, privately?" She stood posed in the doorway, photo-shoot style.

"Of course," Elly responded in wonderment.

Suzie began, speaking slowly at first and then picking up speed, "The day you started, you said if there's a problem we could talk to you any time. I do have some problems in this office, and I need to talk to you about them, very confidentially. Promise me you'll keep it all a secret. Promise me, Elly, or I won't be able to tell you."

"But of course," answered Elly, bracing herself.

"First, I want to tell you about Byron and what happened between us when I first came into the office ten years ago. He's told me on several occasions how attracted he is to me and how he shivers when I come into his office. When I first transferred into the office from the plant, he used to stand real close to me when we spoke, and he still does from time to time. You see, I've always had a problem with my beauty—it has been very difficult for me.

"Well, one time when I was at home, he phoned me. He said he had a fight with his wife and had no place to go. He asked if he could come spend the night with me. Of course, I said no. I told him he did not appeal to me—he had as much appeal as a peanut butter sandwich." She stopped at this point and waited for Elly's reaction.

Elly was careful not to sound patronizing. "I can well imagine how difficult all of that would have been for you. You are a lovely girl, Suzie, and can expect men to be attracted—but remember, your character is far more important than your looks. You're excellent at processing the orders for Sunshine and handling the bookings for the convention center—and customer complaints. And I've noticed you work very well with the Service Department." Elly could see the flush of pride creep into Suzie's fat cheeks and felt disingenuous for thinking, beauty, indeed!

"Thanks for the compliment," Suzie replied. "Speaking of the Service Department, I must tell you I have a pact with Eric Joyble. He created it when I started in the office. He told me if I help him with his job by doing extra things, he'll always stick up for me. I do a lot for him—all his filing and a bunch of other stuff, like handing him customer files. He just hates putting his hand into a file cabinet. He says my help gives him free time to go out for coffee or go shopping whenever he hankers. Byron doesn't know about this arrangement, so please don't tell him—or anyone else. It's the biggest secret of my life!"

"I never break a promise," replied Elly, flabbergasted.

"Oh, one last thing, sometime soon I may look for other employment because I've been extremely bored with Sunshine for a long time. Would you give me a letter of reference?"

"I would be happy to," said Elly, desperately trying to conceal her eagerness.

Without a thank you, Suzie strutted back to her workstation. And before Suzie had a chance to sit down, Elly had a sheet of letterhead in her typewriter, ready to compose the best letter of recommendation she'd ever written.

Now she knew why Suzie lacked respect for her as a supervisor—she did not regard her as such. She refused to take direction from Elly because she had an "in" with a senior manager. In fact, she was under the supervision of no one. It explained a lot of things: why Suzie was conceited and disrespectful, and why Joyble was aloof and unfriendly.

The story Suzie had told her about Mr. Stewart's lack of discretion was puzzling, indeed. Stewart didn't seem the type of man who would take advantage of a staff member, especially not such a young, Asian girl. On the other hand, maybe it was a case of an older man suffering a midlife crisis. Either way, what purpose would knowing whether it was true serve?

There were no more encounters with Eric Joyble. He stayed out of the office for long stretches, claiming to be promoting Sunshine Linen along the coast. When he was in Summergrove, he spent his time on various floors of the convention center, taking care of their linen needs. He had no idea Elly knew about his arrangement with Suzie.

12

Christmas Cheer

The busy atmosphere at Sunshine Linen continued through fall into winter. Elly had been so busy learning her new job and dealing with staff and health problems, she had only recently gotten the opportunity to get to know the other two managers, Alan McCormick, production, and Bob Jones, sales.

Alan McCormick was elderly and suffered from emphysema, always short of breath from climbing the long flight of stairs to the basement, home to the washers, extractors, dryers and the bulk of his staff. Apparently, he found it difficult to control his people and keep them happy. There was a constant stream of employees with some grievance or other passing Elly's door into Mr. Stewart's office. *How distracting and disruptive this must be for production,* thought Elly.

Bob Jones was seldom in the office. Mr. Stewart didn't allow him there past 9:30 A.M. "You're not selling if you're here," he frequently declared. However, that still left plenty of time for Jones to dominate the office area, placing his demands on the staff, especially when he'd just been empowered by a large sale. He was in his early forties, married with two children, but rumors abounded about his infidelities.

Jones was in constant dispute with Suzie over one thing or another, and Joyble always sided with Suzie. In exasperation and with Suzie standing on the sidelines giggling, Jones had complained to Elly, expecting her to take a stand. But Elly's hands were tied. Joyble was a senior manager. She just hoped Suzie would find another job soon. It became a waiting game for Elly, as she struggled to keep peace in the office.

Christmas came without warning, or so it seemed to Mr. Stewart, who was responsible for organizing the Christmas luncheon for the plant workers and office staff. Although he'd cut back considerably on the number of platters and fancy sandwiches ordered from a local restaurant since the strike in the late seventies, it still was essential to provide something for the workers.

This will be the job of the office manager from now on, he decided, relieved to place the task on someone else's shoulders. He phoned Elly, "We usually organize a little something in the way of food for the staff in the lunchroom upstairs … to celebrate Christmas. Could you please look after it?"

"I'd be delighted," replied Elly, welcoming a diversion. "How much can I spend?"

"Well, if I remember correctly, it cost eight dollars per person last year—that was bloody steep! There were assorted sandwiches, some pickles, a platter of pastries and a beverage."

Elly quietly calculated, then replied, "I could cook a delicious baron of beef dinner, complete with all the trimmings, for ten dollars per person." Stewart raised his eyebrows. "We'd only have to rent dishes and chafers. I'm used to cooking for a crowd. My husband and I used to entertain large military groups. It would be a real treat for the employees, Byron, and just might increase production. I could easily do it," she concluded.

"There's no doubt about your ability," Mr. Stewart replied, hiding his astonishment.

It's the precedent I'm concerned with. But go ahead with it— just make certain you coordinate with production for the timing of the dinner. We have to have the trucks loaded before we eat."

Excited about the upcoming dinner, Elly decided it would be fun to provide some entertainment, perhaps a skit put on by the office, so she summoned her staff. They were thrilled about the dinner, but it took some time to convince them to participate in a skit. They finally agreed and decided to perform a skit on the history of Sunshine Linen that Elly would write. The story she had in mind revolved around how things had improved after the corporation hired a British manager, namely Byron Stewart. Elly spent the majority of her lunch hours for the next week writing. When it was finally completed, she and the staff met and read it over a few times, deciding no formal rehearsal would be necessary. They would "wing it," so to speak. "Very often, it's much better that way," Elly agreed, laughing. "I know you'll all be great stars!"

Suzie immediately opted for the part of narrator. Coveralls, a significant commodity at Sunshine, would be the garment depicted in the story, going from shabby, tattered ones to crisp, clean ones. To add a touch of humor, a Union Jack would be sewn on the back of the clean ones. Rita and Melody would be the models. It was all intended to make the staff laugh and give a kind of a backhanded compliment to the general manager as a thank you for the dinner.

The day of the dinner, Elly had risen at 4:00 A.M. to put a large baron of beef in the oven and prepare the balance of the dinner. Melody was in charge of setting up the tables and preparing the lunchroom. The long counter was covered with white linen to hold the rented chafers, with white dinner plates stacked neatly at the far end to designate the starting point of the service. White linen also covered every table, each centered with a Christmas floral arrangement made by Rita. Red napkins folded into fans stood at each place setting.

The buffet began with a basket piled high with whole wheat and white dinner rolls, accompanied by a tub of creamery butter. Next was what Elly considered to be the appetite tantalizer, a platter of pickles arranged around a chrysanthemum she'd carved from a white onion. A large bowl of colorful, crisp vegetables in bite-size pieces—cauliflower, carrots, tomato, black olives, sweet onion and chickpeas in a garlic tinged vinaigrette—followed. The chafers held fluffy mounds of mashed potatoes, rich brown mushroom gravy, golden, corn-kernels accented with diced red peppers, and green beans almandine. Two little bowls of horseradish complemented the luscious baron of beef on a cutting board at the end of the line. For dessert, there were two large bowls of trifle garnished with red cherries and kiwis. The employees could not believe their eyes, and neither could Mr. Stewart. They all ate their fill of everything and went back for seconds. Elly was delighted, especially when Mr. Stewart whispered, "Well done, Ellykins"— apparently a newly assigned pet name—then rose and asked for everyone's attention. He wished all a merry Christmas and then thanked Elly most generously. As everyone in the room stood and clapped, the sound was deafening.

Elly stood and, looking at all the smiling faces while waiting for the commotion to subside, said, "It's been my pleasure. Now, we'll have entertainment momentarily, but first we'll need to prepare the room. Could you please free up some space in the center by moving your tables? Thanks."

Suzie, script in hand and an impish grin playing around the corners of her mouth, plugged in a small tape recorder and was about to begin her narration when Melody's piercing laughter, interspersed with musical giggles from Rita, came echoing up the staircase. Although Suzie had already struck her movie-star pose, ready to begin, upon hearing her co-worker's laughter, she too broke into giggles. The audience, caught up in the mirth, began to laugh, as well.

Elly gazed around the crowded room and thought the moment priceless. Here all the employees sat together, their stomachs filled to the brim with delicious food she'd prepared, and now, for the first time on the job, they were about to be entertained—by the "Ladies of The Office," no less. The ambience was great—the gratification, greater!

Recovering, Suzie coughed and asked for attention, then began to read her lines in a loud, exaggerated voice. "Once upon a time, in the year 1968, Sunshine Linen was experiencing great difficulty in processing their coveralls. They were about to lose the contract with the local mill, until a fine gentleman from England came to the rescue.

"He—this fine gentleman, that is, from England, that is— rode in on a big white stallion, tied his steed to the veranda pole by the back door, scurried down the stairs to the washing machines and, in a flash, changed the soap formula. He changed it to his very own secret one, a secret he brought across the ocean and one he holds to this day. Not only did his secret formula turn out the whitest table linen for this convention center, but the cleanest coveralls for the mill anyone could ever have imagined! He saved the contract that was about to collapse.

"Now, ladies and gentlemen, just feast your eyes on the perfection of this laundered coverall, the product of the formula from this fine man from England who rode in on his white stallion and tied it to the pole of the veranda and scurried downstairs."

Hey, wait a minute! There must be a mistake. That's supposed to be in the second part of the skit—that's supposed to be the conclusion. Now I understand why they've been giggling. They've changed it, the little stinkers! Elly thought. She glanced over at Mr. Stewart, who was smiling and obviously getting a big kick out of it all.

Then Suzie started the music, "Winchester Cathedral," and in marched Rita, tall and slim in a brand-new pair of coveralls as she half-skipped, half-marched around the crowded room to the music. She did a double step when she passed Mr. Stewart and feigned a curtsy. Everyone was giggling and pointing at the Union Jack on the back of the coveralls. Rita skipped out of the room to applause and shouts of "Yea, yea!"

"Now let's see how the garments looked before the savior from England came galloping in to tie his horse to the pole, etcetera, etcetera, etcetera," mocked Suzie as she pressed the play button on the tape recorder.

As Elly heard the opening line, "I've got a lovely bunch of coconuts," she leaned toward Mr. Stewart and exclaimed, "That's not the song I selected! They've totally changed the skit. I wonder what they're up to!" Then Melody appeared in the oiliest, most tattered pair of size 54 coveralls the ladies could find, backing her way into the room, gyrating her hips to the rhythm of the song. When she turned around, the audience screamed with laughter. Hanging down between her legs was a huge stuffed penis with a red Christmas bulb flashing at its tip, swinging to and fro as she sidestepped to "big ones, small ones, some as big as your fist."

If there had been a crack in the floor, Elly would have gladly slithered into it. But once over the initial shock and embarrassment, she could see the humor in their prank. What a sight it was—a two-hundred-pound woman dancing with this grotesque appendage pinned between her legs! What a sport Melody was!

Later while scooping generous portions of roast beef, mashed potatoes, gravy and vegetables from the chafing dishes onto a large aluminum pie plate, Mr. Stewart walked over to Elly and asked, "Is the playwright actually still hungry?"

"Oh, no," laughed Elly, patting her stomach. "This is for Sammy.

"Sammy?"

"He's the smokie vendor on the corner every morning. He must be awfully tired of eating them for lunch. And by the way, Byron, just so there's no misunderstanding, I wrote the play but definitely wasn't in charge of the costumes."

"I guessed as much," he replied. "But I have to admit, it was hilarious!"

Elly arrived at the corner just in time to see Sammy stepping into the van to drive away. "Wait, Sammy! Don't leave! I've got something for you, here," she shouted Elly. "I thought you might enjoy some roast beef for a change."

"Golly, thanks, Elly! Roast beef—that'll be a real treat!" Although his blue eyes twinkled with genuine gratitude, they were puffy, and his chubby little face looked tired and drawn.

When they were leaving the building that night, Mr. Stewart reminded Elly about the next night's Christmas dinner for managers and their spouses. "Be at the restaurant at 6:30 P.M., sharp," he commanded.

She was restless all day Saturday, anxiously waiting for the event. It would be her first chance to meet the spouses of the other managers. At four o'clock, she ran her bath and then carefully chose her outfit, a slim-fitting black dress, black shoes and hose, plus a glitter pin for her shoulder with earrings to match. Always disappointed with her own short fingernails she even put on an artificial set painted hot pink. "How do I look?" she asked Vincent.

"You look just fine," he replied. "Why the excitement, Elly, we're not going to Buckingham Palace to visit the queen."

"I want to look my best, dear. This is our first dinner party with all the managers and their wives, and I hear the place we're going is quite something!"

When he first arrived at Sunshine Linen, Mr. Stewart had secured a standing reservation for his staff's Christmas dinner with the Harbor Lights Restaurant. He did it for three reasons: they used only Sunshine linens; their seasonal decorations were elaborate; and they served the best food in town. Christmas was always special and tonight was no exception.

After they had given their coats to the maitre 'd, Elly's first impression was a roomful of finely dressed patrons in animated conversation at candlelit tables. Then she noticed the bright red blossoms of large potted geraniums lined against the walls and wondered why they sparkled. Realizing tiny lights had been hidden among their leaves, she thought, *How effective! I'll have to remember that one.* Additional lights in assorted colors framed the windows, shimmering onto the still water of the harbor. It truly was a festive and beautiful place for a dinner party.

Elly had to scan the room several times before she recognized the Sunshine Linen group seated at a long table. The metamorphosis rendered by their dress clothes made them hard to pick out in the low light. *They're all here—they must've come early,* she thought.

After the spousal introductions, Elly and Vincent took the two vacant spaces at the end of the table. This placed Vincent next to McCormick, the elderly production manager, and Elly—much to her chagrin—next to Bob Jones, the flirtatious sales manager. He flashed his white teeth and declared in a loud voice, "You're looking lovely tonight!"

"Nice of you to say so," responded Elly curtly, and then turned her attention to studying her colleagues' partners. Eric and his pixie-like wife, Lucy, sat together in the middle, directly across from Mr. Stewart and his wife. Obviously, this was the place of honor. Jones's attractive, dark-haired wife was seated on Mr. Stewart's other side, exchanging one-liners, pun after pun, while others vied for his attention.

As the dinner arrived, Mr. Stewart picked up his napkin and said, "We can definitely be proud of this lovely table linen. It looks like my secret formula is working extremely well." He winked at Elly. Lobster and steak, the most expensive item on the menu, was the dinner choice of everyone. Nothing satisfies the palate of a seafood lover more than well-prepared lobster, and everyone responded to Mr. Stewart's ongoing jokes with hearty laughter. But his wife's excessive laughter indicated she was well into the alcohol before everyone arrived. She was a small woman with heavy features, so short she didn't even reach Mr. Stewart's shoulders, and she became progressively louder as the evening went on, Mr. Stewart having to hush her on a couple occasions. It was clear to Elly that Mr. Stewart not only controlled his plant but also his dinner parties.

As the evening progressed, the subject of grandchildren arose. Eric and Lucy said they didn't want grandchildren, referring to them as rug rats. They said they were happy now that their kids had grown up and left—now their home was theirs and theirs alone. "Do your children visit often?" inquired Elly, trying to participate in the conversation.

"Oh, yes, when we invite them," replied Eric. "But we don't allow any overnights." He seemed proud of the stand he'd taken with his children.

How sad for the children! Elly thought, casting her gaze down and noticing something pink on the table near her plate. To her horror, she realized it was one of her artificial nails and quickly hid it in her evening bag.

Unfortunately, it did not go unnoticed by Jones, who shouted, "Hey, everyone, look here! Our new office manager is falling apart!" Everyone's attention turned to a mortified Elly, just in time to see a second nail fall off. Although her fingernails were the source of a lot of laughter the rest of the night, Elly reminded herself there were worse things in life one could be embarrassed about.

The following day, Elly sent a thank-you card to the Stewarts, saying how much she and Vincent had enjoyed the dinner. Two days later, a smiling Mr. Stewart walked into her office and said, "Sally and I opened our mail over breakfast this morning, and we had a good laugh when a couple of your fingernails fell out of the card!"

"Mission accomplished!" Elly replied, her laughter ringing out like Christmas bells.

13

Sheep's Clothing

Before winter was over, all the typewriters in the office had been replaced by personal computers. Although most of the staff was befuddled by this amazing new technology, Rita adapted quickly, hardly a day going by that Elly didn't marvel at her efficiency. Suzie also was quick to learn the new techniques, but Melody had problems catching on. After several attempts to prepare a small spreadsheet, she ran from the room crying. A plant worker who saw her in the bathroom informed Elly.

"I hate change," Melody sobbed, her face red and tear-stained.

"Change will always be with us, Melody. That's one thing we can be sure of," comforted Elly, her arm not quite reaching all the way across Melody's shoulders. "In the future, come and talk to me for a few minutes when you're exasperated. Just remember to take your time when you're working with the computer. Computer work is sequential."

"I hate being so dumb! Everyone looks at me and thinks I'm not only fat but dumb, too!" She sobbed again and blew her nose.

"No, Melody, that's not true. When people look at you, they see Melody, a kind and loving person. Anyone looking at you differently doesn't matter a lick! Now, let's go back to your desk and attack that monster. You know the old saying, 'Two heads are better than one.' Now, let's get out of this bathroom!"

Back at the desk, Elly could follow what Melody was doing and saw that she was rushing and missing a step. "Go slowly, Melody. It has to be exact, just like a telephone number," she encouraged. After a few more attempts, Melody managed to get it right. "Clear the screen and repeat it three more times, then it will be yours. And try to remember how you did it—you may have to show me one day!" Elly laughed.

Another new invention came right on the heels of the computer, a fax machine. It also had everyone marveling, amazed at the ability to send a letter in just a few minutes. It also was amazing to Elly how people rose to meet the challenge of advancing technology, all of which would become "old hat" in due course. But changes of a different kind also were afoot.

One morning, Mr. Stewart buzzed Elly on the phone, "Please come to my office straightaway. I need to discuss something important."

"I'll be right in," Elly replied, dropping her work and hurrying into his office, notepad in hand.

"Alan McCormick has just given me his notice—he says it's doctor's orders. I'm going to have to hire a new production manager, but first I need you to check into our disability pension to see exactly what kind of coverage he'll receive. He's not a man of means."

"I'll do that right away, Byron," she responded, with a mental image of McCormick gasping at the top of the stairs. She was pleased Mr. Stewart showed concern. "But isn't this going to leave you in a bit of a lurch? Who's going to supervise production?"

"At first, I'd planned to look after production myself until I engaged someone new, but I guess this is my lucky day. A manager from another branch, anxious to move to Summergrove, has agreed to start next Monday. His name is Joe Billington. I've met him casually in the past, and he's seems like a bright bloke." Mr. Stewart had harbored doubts about Alan McCormick's health for some time, expecting that, sooner or later, he'd have to replace him. And now with Billington, everything seemed to have worked out quite well.

Joe Billington leaned back in his cushioned chair, put his feet on top of his desk and stared into space. He couldn't remember when he'd felt so good about himself. Being handpicked by Byron Stewart as his new production manager in the little town of Summergrove couldn't have come at a better time. *"Handpicked!" Not transferred, but "handpicked!" Life just doesn't get any better!* He was anxious to move. Far too many people were pursuing him for money, far too much hassling going on, especially from his ex-wife.

Now he could leave it all behind—instruct the loyal office staff not to disclose his whereabouts, get an unlisted phone number—and start a new life, thanks to Byron Stewart. He was also happy to leave the job of office manager behind—all those audits drove him crazy. The only perk had been easy access to cash whenever he needed it. It was so easy to take a case of toilet tissue to a customer and collect the money. And he'd heard that the new office manager at Sunshine in Summergrove was a woman. She'd be a pushover.

He admired the wall where he had arranged all his soccer pictures in a neat row. Now forty-eight, he could only reflect upon them with melancholy as the "good old days." *I was a damn good player, the best on the team. They would never have gotten those awards without me.* Of a stocky build, Joe Billington was short by most standards, and his black hair had long since turned grey. But despite his gapped, beaver-like teeth, he never had trouble getting a woman, usually a clandestine meeting with one of the foreign employees, who felt important dating a manager.

When he laughed, he would shuffle his feet and put his big teeth on display, sparking laughter all around. Life really was one big joke to him, a stage on which he was the main actor, using his intelligence, wit and humor to get anything he wanted. This often meant developing allies, as he had with the general manager of the laundry he was leaving. Billington had saved his hide when the head office investigated and accused him of using company money to build his house. Coming to his rescue, Billington had proved otherwise, establishing a lifelong indebtedness.

There was nothing, he had convinced himself, he couldn't do and nothing he couldn't get if he set his mind to it—like how he had used the tip he got from his drinking buddy Oscar, who used to sell real estate. "You don't need to put any money down, my friend," Oscar had told him. "All you do is find a seller who's desperate—if he's desperate enough, he'll give you a phony receipt. You produce this phony receipt to the bank to show you already made the down payment, and they'll approve your mortgage, just like that!" That was exactly what he had done when he hit Summergrove. The thought of pulling off that little caper made him exceedingly thirsty. He got up, stretched and headed out of his new office for the bar, leaving a rank odor in his wake.

Elly had been observing Billington with interest since his arrival at Sunshine—he looked like such a fun-loving character, with his happy face and beaver smile. When Mr. Stewart had taken him around for introductions, they visited her office last so she could complete paperwork for his personnel file. As he stood in her doorway, he gave her a military salute.

"What was that for?" she asked, bemused.

"Just being respectful—I hear you're the general around this place." He laughed.

Elly laughed, too—he looked so comical, standing there at attention with his foolish, toothy grin. *He's going to be a lot of fun,* she decided.

When the paperwork was finished, Billington shifted in his chair and proudly stated, "I'm in the process of buying a house. Do you know of a good realtor?"

Elly remembered an elderly woman who had just lost her husband and was trying her hand at real estate. Having her first client would give her a boost. "I sure do," she replied. "Her name is Jane and she works for Summergrove Realty. Actually, it's adjacent to this center, immediately to the left. That'd be convenient."

"I'll head over there right now. Oh, another small thing—I'm completely without furniture, not even a chair to put my sorry butt on." He laughed. "Are there any cheap secondhand stores where I could pick up some stuff, like a chesterfield, bed ... table? All I have ... let's see ..." He closed his eyes momentarily as he calculated. "All I have is two hundred dollars to spend."

"I know of several secondhand places, all within a four-block radius," replied Elly. "They're certain to have what you need."

"Would you be able to drive me around to check them out during lunch hour? My car is being repaired this afternoon. Sorry, I don't mean to be such a pest."

"Sure," said Elly. "I'd be happy to accommodate you."

True to her word, they spent the lunch hour shopping, selecting a bed, chest of drawers, table, chair, and sagging brown sofa.

When they got back to the office, Billington said, "Oh, I just realized I forgot to pick up some pots and dishes. Damn, I have only two bucks left!"

"What is it you need, exactly?" asked Elly.

"Oh, I'm a simple kind of guy—all I require is an old frying pan to scramble my eggs, a pot to boil spaghetti, a plate to eat it on and a fork and knife—ya know, just enough to get by.

I have some extra cutlery and odd cooking utensils in the basement at home I have no use for. I'll bring some things in for you tomorrow."

Within the next three days, Billington had moved his second-hand furniture and Elly's utensils into his new condo. And within three more days, he'd rented his extra bedrooms to men he'd met in the bar. Their rent money covered the mortgage and utilities, leaving his entire paycheck for him to enjoy.

Several weeks passed before Elly discovered that Joe Billington wasn't the man he seemed. Noticing that he'd been hanging around Melody's desk more than necessary, putting his arm around her plump shoulder and engaging her in private whispering sessions, Elly suddenly thought, I *wonder if he's approached Melody for money from the petty cash. All this attentiveness is flattering to Melody and he knows it—he also knows she's the sole custodian of the cash box.*

Fearing the worst, Elly asked Melody to come into her office. "This is strictly confidential, Melody. I need to ask you something very, very important. And please know, Melody, it'll just be between the two of us."

"Of course!" Melody loved a secret and her eyes sparkled in anticipation.

Elly went right to the point, her gaze unwavering, "Has Joe borrowed any money from you, Melody?"

Melody sat up straight in her chair and flushed. "Promise me you'll keep it a secret, too," she pleaded.

"You know I will," answered Elly.

"Yes, he did borrow a small amount—the second week after he arrived. He said he was desperate." Melody fidgeted in her chair, rubbing her palms together. "He promised to pay me back—he just hasn't been able to yet. But I know he will—he looks like an honest gentleman."

Horrified, Elly asked, "How much did he borrow, Melody?"

"Only fifty dollars," she stammered.

"Fifty dollars Melody, that's a lot of money! Did he give you a receipt or sign something?"

"Why should he sign anything?" replied Melody, looking perplexed. "He's a manager."

"You know the rules for petty cash. Manager or no manager, corporate policies apply to everyone." Elly saw embarrassment coupled with fear in Melody's eyes and felt a wave of compassion.

"Oh, it wasn't from petty cash. It was from me, personally. He only borrowed twenty dollars from petty cash."

"You mean he borrowed money from you, personally, and from petty cash?" Elly's voice had risen.

"Yes," said Melody, averting her eyes.

Sensitive to her situation, Elly empathized with the pitiful woman seated in front of her desk. "Look, Melody, I know you are a kind-hearted lady. I know you'd give anyone the shirt off your back. But loaning it without really knowing if you'll get it back just isn't fair to you—you work hard for your money. I can't tell you what to do with your personal money, but promise me you will think about this."

"I will," murmured Melody, hanging her head.

"The petty cash, Melody, is a different story altogether. It is corporate money. Personal loans from the cash box are strictly forbidden. I can't stress that enough!"

As she watched Melody's dejected frame fill the doorway as she returned to her desk, she wondered how long it would take her to realize Billington's attention was flattery with a purpose. Knowing there was nothing she could do at present, she resolved to keep a close eye on Billington in the future. In the meantime, she waited until he was in earshot and then asked Melody for the petty cash box. Sure enough, there was a chit for twenty dollars with his name on it.

Now Elly could speak to him about borrowing company money without breaking her promise to Melody. "I saw a chit in petty cash for twenty dollars with your signature on it," Elly said. "No one is allowed to borrow from petty cash, a company's strict rule. I've instructed Melody never to lend from it to anyone—and that includes managers. You can either pay it back to me tomorrow or I can show it as a deduction from your pay. It's better for you to just pay it back. Head office scrutinizes the payroll and would be certain to question the deduction."

He stared at her through yellow-tinged eyes, searching for a clever retort but unable to find one. "I'll give you the cash," he snarled, taking a twenty-dollar bill out of his pocket and slamming it down on her desk.

As he left, Elly knew she had made an enemy. Now she really would have to be on guard. And on guard she was, all summer long. Some days, Billington came in to work bright and cheerful. Other days, he was puffy-eyed and sullen, spending the day in his office with the door half open. During these times, he was intentionally uncooperative, refusing to give Elly the inventory count and approval of his department's invoices for payment. *It's as if he's punishing me for keeping his fingers out of the petty cash box,* thought Elly, *but if that's what it takes to keep him honest, so be it.*

And during these times, a noxious odor of garlic and vomit seeped from his pores and spread down the long hallway into the main office. All the staff complained and covered their mouths when they went by his door. Finally, Mr. Stewart spoke to him, standing in his doorway with the back of his hand against his mouth, "Where the hell's that unforgivable stench coming from, Billington?"

"I don't smell anything," Billington declared, looking around.

"Do something about it," Mr. Stewart retorted.

Billington promptly placed air fresheners around the room to camouflage the odor, but although it took the edge off the odor, a nauseating trace remained.

Elly paid regular visits to Rita in the computer room to discuss her concerns about Billington. She was happy to have another woman who viewed things in the same light to talk to. And it was Rita who was the first to tell Elly that a driver's packet of COD money containing over five hundred dollars was missing this Tuesday morning. "I know Melody's going to come in and talk to you about it, but I want to warn you first," said Rita, her brown eyes clouded with concern.

"Thanks Rita, I won't reveal you've told me. Oh, my goodness, over five hundred dollars! That's serious, real serious." Immediately, she thought of Billington and wondered if he was guilty—and how he could have stolen it. She knew the drivers turned in the cash to Melody at day's end. Melody then counted it in front of them, placed it in the safe and locked the door—it was a ritual she'd been performing for years.

A short time later, Melody came in and, between sobs, blurted out the story, "I just can't figure out how it could disappear overnight. I counted the money, put the packet in the safe and locked the door last night before I went home, just as sure as I'm sitting here, and this morning it's gone!"

Elly handed her a tissue and asked, "Is there the slightest chance you left it on your desk, intending to put in it the safe? That could happen to anyone, Melody, especially if there's an interruption by someone. There are so many people, including the public, coming in to pick up their last-minute linens, constantly walking past your desk."

"No, I would never do that. I'm a creature of habit. I would never forget to put the money in the safe."

"And here's another scenario—did you, perhaps, put it in the safe and not lock the door, purely by accident?"

"No, as I've said, I'm a creature of habit. I've been doing this job for years, the same ritual every day. It's never happened before." She continued to sob, and Elly handed her another tissue.

"Please don't cry, Melody," Elly soothed. "Just keep on guard. Be very careful—double check what you do when handling cash and never leave your desk if you have money out. Never trust any one, not a solitary soul. Now, please go back to your desk and try to put this horrible thing out of your mind. I will make an entry in the journal to remove the amount from the day's sales. And remember, you don't trust anyone—not anyone—ever!"

There was someone Elly didn't trust, but she couldn't do a thing about it. Although she knew Billington was somehow involved with the missing money, she had no proof. It was much too soon to bring it to Mr. Stewart's attention—she needed to gather more evidence, more incidents.

14

A Step Forward, Two Back

Saturday morning, Vincent and the twins left early to go fishing, and Elly slept in until ten. When she awoke, she lay cozily under the covers, contemplating the past workweek. She remembered Darryl Simcoe's embezzlement and Mr. Stewart's note on her first day of work about being the protector of corporate funds. The responsibility lay heavily on her mind.

And the "missing money" issue had put her behind in balancing the bank statement. The filing had also piled up, and Mr. Stewart was waiting for her to check the current expenses against the budget. The more she thought about all the things that needed doing, the more she felt she should slip down to the office to catch up. Her family was away fishing and wouldn't be missing her, so why not use the day to buy some peace of mind? She pulled on a pair of jeans and a sweat top and headed out the door, planning to swing by McDonald's for a quick breakfast.

It was unusual to find the main office door unlocked, but she surmised the janitor was doing his weekend work. As she walked down the hall, she saw Billington at his desk with a mountain of quarters piled in the middle of it. With shaking fingers, he was hastily wrapping them in brown paper rolls.

She paused in his doorway, and when he looked up, he didn't bat an eye. "I'm just rolling my silly old quarters. What are you doing here on a Saturday, general? Don't you have housework to do?"

"I could ask the same of you. And why are you explaining why you're here? What you do on a Saturday is your business, Joe," she replied. As she walked on to her office, she felt certain he was up to no good.

She spent the following two hours completing her office tasks and was relieved to have them behind her, but on the drive home, she found she couldn't get Billington off her mind. *Why did he have to pay a clandestine visit to the office to roll his quarters? Strange, too, that he had such a quantity—he must have been saving them for a mighty long time to acquire such a pile!*

Monday mornings always came too quickly for Elly, but she felt better about going into work this Monday because she had caught up on all her work and could concentrate on processing payments to the suppliers. As she passed Sammy, his plump smokies all lined up on the top grill turning brown and smoking. She said, "Hi there, Sammy! How's the world treating you these days?" She noticed his arm while he was turning his sausages. He was wearing a very expensive looking gold watch. She wondered if it were genuine.

"Couldn't be better!" he lied. Actually, he'd been feeling dreadful the last few days. But Elly was magic—she always cheered him up. And she was the only person in the whole building that acknowledged his presence.

For Elly, the next half hour brought two unwelcome surprises. First, she discovered that the statement from the coffee supplier, normally a break-even situation, showed a large amount owing—two hundred and thirty-seven dollars. And then, Elly received a phone call from a courier demanding payment for an amount over ninety days old.

She decided to deal with the coffee bill first and called them, "I cannot understand why we are invoiced for this amount," she said. "You put the coffee in, and the employees pay a quarter for every cup. It has to be a "break-even" situation." The minute she said the word "quarter," a sick feeling came over her.

"I'll speak to the man who services your machine with coffee and collects the quarters," she was told politely, "and I'll call you back. Sometimes, when he's with customers, he's difficult to reach, but just as soon as I'm able to contact him, I'll get back to you." True to her word, within a few minutes, she called back, "The service rep told me that when he emptied your machine last week, there were very few quarters in it. He wondered about it at the time."

"Thank you for being so prompt," said Elly before hanging up and calling about the courier bill. After asking their head office to fax a copy of the signed bill of lading, she asked Rita, in charge of faxed memos, to bring it directly into her office when it arrived. She didn't want it landing with other faxes on Billington's desk.

Sure enough, the bill of lading showed the merchandise was shipped from New York, cost $582.00 and was picked up and signed for by none other than Joe Billington. She compared the signature to the one he signed on his tax exemption form, and they matched exactly. The shipper was not a supplier but a lady, whose name Elly recognized as his latest girlfriend. They'd met at the last managers' Christmas dinner.

Elly finally had had enough. First, there was the money taken from petty cash and the borrowing from Melody, then the missing COD cash, and now the quarters from the coffee machine and this shipping bill charged to the company. It was high time to speak with Mr. Stewart.

"Blimey, I'm just coasting to retirement! I don't feel like dealing with this kind of vexation, not now," lamented Mr. Stewart, suddenly appearing older than his sixty-three years. "I've known for some time he's got a giant problem with the booze, but I certainly didn't think it would come to this." He gestured to the evidence laid out on his desk and sighed heavily. When he raised his eyes, he could see anxiety in Elly's face. "But I realize I have to do something."

Elly could see and feel his despair. To realize one had hand-picked a thief and placed him in charge of a valuable inventory and numerous employees was a bitter pill to swallow.

"We have to be extremely careful with a predicament like this, Elly. We have to be prudent. He can declare he didn't take the driver's money packet, and he can declare he was rolling quarters he'd brought from his home. He can also declare we can't prove a damn thing. And you know something? He'd be accurate. And whatever his declaration, no doubt it would be delivered with a great deal of indignation.

"Now, the shipment for his girlfriend is an entirely different situation, much less complex. The bill of lading bears his signature and try as he might, there isn't any way he can wriggle out of that one. Just leave it rest with me. Thanks for bringing it to my attention and, in the meantime, remain on guard!" He stood up, towering over her slight figure, his cue their conversation was over.

Shortly after, Mr. Stewart's voice came over the intercom, ordering Billington to his office. He had to pass Elly's window, so she saw him go in and was watching for him to come out. It seemed an eternity, but when he finally emerged, he gave Elly a devious glance. He knew she'd spoken to Bryon, and a sense of dread engulfed her.

What was said that afternoon she'd never know. She didn't feel it appropriate to ask, and Mr. Stewart never told her. But whatever the reprimand, it was effective. There were no more phone calls from the courier, no more quarters missing from the coffee machine and, thus far, no more missing cash. Other small issues that appeared fishy popped up time after time, but once again there was "no proof."

Elly was learning that light-fingered petty thieves are the hardest to catch and kept a constant vigil over the cash and assets of the company, but she found it was distracting her from her work.

The role of "protector of corporate funds" had taken on a whole new meaning. *Just tighten up security, do your best and get on with managing the office,* she kept telling herself. *Eventually, one way or the other, he'll cook his own goose!*

She decided, once again, not to tell any of this to Vincent. It would just be too hard on him, now that he was getting older, and would only add to his long list of things to worry about. But she couldn't help recalling, as she'd done so often in the past, how he'd warned her all those years ago to watch out for the cutthroats, backstabbers and thieves. And she couldn't help feeling proud that her latest experiences, along with some of the earlier ones, had shown she could meet those devils head on.

Melody was exhausted as she drove home that Thursday afternoon. It was month end and, as usual, delinquent customers had flooded in with their payments. And she had found it difficult to keep up with Rita who needed the payment sheet for data entering. It had been nothing but rush, rush, rush, all day long. As she finished the second of the two stale donuts she found left in her car, a troubling question entered her weary mind: *Did I lock the safe?*

Heart thumping, she mentally retraced her steps. She recalled walking to the safe and placing the huge deposit of cash and checks inside for banking the following morning. Then Billington had called her to the hallway. She could hear her own laughter in her mind at his joke, but she couldn't remember a thing beyond his interruption. Frantic, she thought, *I won't sleep all night. I'd better hurry back and check it!* Making an illegal u-turn, she sped back to the office.

As she entered, she noticed Billington working late in his office. *A rare happening,* she thought—she'd often seen him disappear out the backdoor early. She hurried across to the small room that housed the safe. Testing the safe's heavy iron door, she was shocked when it swung open. *My God, how could I have been so careless?* She quickly checked the money packet and was relieved to find everything intact. "Thank goodness, I double checked it! What a blessed relief that is!"

If it had been missing, she would've rather killed herself then face Elly and Mr. Stewart with news of another loss. She slammed the safe door shut with a clang and jiggled the handle to make sure the lock had caught, the sounds resonating through the building. Then she walked slowly back down the long hallway, noting the lingering bleach odor she had been too worried to notice when she'd entered. "Good night, Joe!" she called as she passed his odorous doorway.

He didn't answer—he was preoccupied. The slamming of the safe door was still ringing in his ears, his throat was parched and his hands were shaking. He was flat broke, with no prospects. But he'd find a way.

The next morning, Elly was greeted at the door by an excited Rita, "I came in early today, and the janitor stopped me in the hall and told me we were robbed last night!"

Elly's heart fell. "Robbed, how … how much?" she exclaimed, trembling.

"Someone broke a window then robbed the coffee machine—pried it open and took every quarter. The machine is badly bent, but I don't think there was much in there—maybe fifty dollars max, according to Joe Billington."

"He couldn't possibly know how much it contained," Elly said. "Byron took the key away from him. The coffee distributor has the only key, now, which he uses once a month to service it. I wonder how he can declare it was only fifty dollars."

"I wondered that, too," replied Rita. "But that's what the man said."

"What window was broken?"

"The one in the upstairs closet adjacent to the lunchroom, you know where the janitor keeps his cleaning supplies. He says no one could possibly know the small window was there unless they're familiar with the building. He thinks it must have been a past employee."

"Do you know if Joe called the police?" Elly asked.

"Yes, he did. I overheard him tell them not to bother coming out because it really was a small incident," replied Rita.

"Really," Elly exclaimed. "I find that strange. You'd think they'd want to retrieve some fingerprints. I've heard them say break-ins in a neighborhood are often done by the same individual. Well, I guess we better get to work. I'll inform Byron about it when he comes in. But in the meantime, I'm going to see where that window is."

Sure enough, at the back of the janitor supply room, a small window was broken. It appeared to have been broken from the inside—all the glass was on the roof, something a policeman would have picked up on immediately.

When she encountered Billington in the hallway later, she purposely widened her eyes and said, "I hear we were broken into last night and money was stolen from the coffee machine."

"These things happen in business, Elly," he responded. The odor of his alcohol-soaked breath hung in the close hallway, and the look in his bloodshot eyes told her he knew he wasn't fooling her.

Suzie, whose behavior had been unusually low key lately, was euphoric this morning. She'd received a call from a bank manager in a nearby town the night before, offering her the position of secretary to the manager, a job she had applied for the previous week. She hadn't expected to be hired, but she had noticed how attracted to her the manager seemed to be, which had pleased her immensely. *I think I'll tell Eric first, then the girls here in the office, then the people in the plant and, then, I'll tell Elly, in that order.*

Within seconds of hearing the news, Rita had told Elly. Within ten minutes, everyone in the building knew Suzie had accepted a new job and would be leaving in two weeks. Later, right at closing time, Elly noticed Suzie loitering around her doorway—she knew why.

Suzie approached her as Elly was donning her coat and announced, "I've got a new job! I'll be leaving two weeks from Monday."

"Really?" said Elly, feigning surprise.

"Where?"

"At the big, new bank in Bakersfield."

Suzie grinned widely and added, "It's a job with a whole lot more class than Sunshine could ever dream of having."

"That will be a challenge for you!" responded Elly. "I hope you'll be happy there. In the morning, put your resignation in the form of a letter, please, so it can be placed in your file."

"I think that can be managed," Suzie said tartly, a ring of triumph in her voice, and strutted out of the office, chest up and hips swaying.

At long last, the conspiracy between Eric Joyble and Suzie would be over. Elly couldn't have gotten better news and mused that it must have been the letter of recommendation she wrote. Dismissing any feelings of remorse she might have had about misleading them, she thought, *I know the bank won't put up with any of her shenanigans!*

Two weeks later, the day after Suzie's departure, Rita beckoned Elly into the computer room, her eyes dancing with mischief. "You won't believe what Suzie did yesterday before she left!" Rita giggled in her musical way. "Brace yourself!"

"I'm braced," Elly replied anxiously.

"I don't know if I can tell you—it's just too bizarre!" Rita laughed again and buried her head in her arms on her desk.

"Hurry up and tell me!" Elly said, joining in her contagious laughter. "Please don't hold me in suspense a moment longer."

"OK, then, here goes," said Rita, lowering her voice to a husky whisper, "Suzie went into Byron's office right before she left and spit right on the middle of his desk, right where he lays his morning newspaper."

"She did what?" Elly exclaimed, her hand flying to her mouth. "Was he there?"

That mental image made Rita throw back her head and laugh all the louder. "No, he wasn't there. Oh, my God, that would have been just too funny! No, he must have been down the hall or somewhere."

Thank goodness! How could anyone do such a horrid thing?" Elly recalled the glowing letter of recommendation she'd given Suzie and was even happier she'd written it. "Thank God, she's gone!" Now, just maybe, she would have to learn to behave, the lesson Joyble prevented Elly from giving her.

The ad in the paper for Suzie's position had drawn numerous applicants, the screening and a job unto itself. It was difficult to decide whom to choose since all the women were equally qualified. Elly finally based her selection on need. Since Carlita Gonzales, thirty-two, was the only single lady among the five finalists, Elly presumed she was in the greatest need of a job and hired her.

On Carlita's first day alone on the job, after a two-week training period with Suzie, Elly noticed that Joyble was lingering in the office longer than usual and was crestfallen when she noticed him escort Carlita into his office and shut the door. *Oh, no, here we go again!*

From that point on, Carlita was sullen and didn't blend well with her co-workers or the flow of business. Rita said she didn't like Carlita one little bit. Elly agreed that she was moody but, nonetheless, intelligent and with a much better disposition than Suzie. She hoped it would all work out, Joyble or no Joyble.

15

The Devil You Know

Three copies of Elly's typewritten note were hand-delivered to Messers Eric Joyble, service manager; Bob Jones, sales manager; and Joe Billington, production manager:

Gentlemen,
Please come to my office at 1:30 P.M. today
for a very important meeting.
Elly

She had purposely kept the topic of the meeting a mystery, knowing no one would come if she told them. She also knew curiosity would be a draw. Proving her reasoning correct, each of Elly's colleagues arrived at the appointed time, led by Joyble, slim, slick and neat

Although he was usually out of the office, Joyble continued to cause problems for Elly. How could she supervise a staff member who was in cahoots with her superior? She was tempted to approach Mr. Stewart with the problem, but she knew Joyble was much harder to replace then she was. In fact, Mr. Stewart had said office managers were a dime a dozen when he hired her. And she needed her job to help her sons in their medical studies. So, she didn't say a word.

As Joyble entered her office, he hoped she wasn't going to ask him for anything. He'd given the company the sweat off his back when he was a driver more than twenty years ago. Now, he was finally comfortable in his job, able to go out anytime he pleased, thanks to having taught the receptionists, first Suzie and now Carlita, to handle service calls on his behalf. Next was Joe Billington, and Elly thought she'd never seen him looking so unhealthy, his face bloated, his skin yellow and his eyes puffy. Nonetheless, he had a roguish look, and Elly wondered what he might be up to now. Bob Jones brought up the rear, flashing his smile. Although Elly always declined his frequent lunch invitations, he had kept right on trying, and Elly assumed it was this insistent aspect of his character that made him such an excellent salesman.

Jones was the first to speak, "What gives? I've got a client to meet."

"Well—" Elly began.

Before she could continue, Billington broke in and announced, his beaver grin spreading across his face, "I'm going to a wedding!"

"Someone in Sunshine getting married?" asked Joyble.

"Me!" Billington declared. "I just thought I would give the baby a name."

"Baby!" exclaimed Joyble. "Whose baby?"

"My baby," said Billington, his grin had turned into a deep throaty chuckle. "It's due in three months."

"My God, Billington, you're old enough to be the child's grandfather!" Jones exclaimed and exchanged a knowing glance with Joyble, disgusted.

Elly broke the silence that followed, "Well, now, there is nothing in this whole world that gives life more purpose than a child."

She glanced at Joyble and then at Billington, who looked grateful. "Now, lets get on with the meeting," she said. "There are a couple of things I need to discuss with you. First, since our last acquisition, the workload has increased significantly in the office, so I've employed another lady. She mainly will be responsible for payroll and benefits—and the rental of the wedding linens. She's starting on Monday, and her name is Anastasia, but she goes by Anna. I'm sure you will all enjoy having her here—she was a lucky find.

"But my main reason for calling the meeting concerns Byron. He's retiring next month, and we need to plan his retirement party. Does anyone know what the protocol is for a retiring general manager?"

"We haven't had one retire before, at least, not since I've been here," said Joyble. "But when your predecessor left, we took him to lunch. I honestly don't believe Byron deserves a whole lot more—he's been awfully mean to me over the years."

"He deserves more than a lunch," said Billington, still smiling. Elly thought he just might be inebriated.

"Yeah," said Jones, "at least, a dinner. Maybe we could invite some of the businessmen I'm trying to sell to right now—may just be the perfect opportunity for me to close the deal."

"Come on, guys!" said Elly. "Let's give him a real party. It'll be a lot fun! This company hasn't had a real "happening" since I've been here. Remember, Byron has held this company together for years. Maybe he hasn't always been in the best of humor—I know we've all witnessed his dark side—but he deserves a whole lot more than a lunch or dinner." Waiting for someone to speak, she decided a little white lie couldn't hurt. "You know, Byron has always had only the nicest things to say about each one of you guys."

"What did you have in mind?" asked Joyble.

"Do you all really want to know?"

"Yeah," they replied alternately. "Well, the local arena, for starters, with limousine service to and from his home, a dinner, a dance, town dignitaries, head office big shots, a short speech by each of us managers and a gift from us all. Now, wouldn't that be something? Wouldn't that give him something to remember when he's old and gray?" Elly enthused, her enormous eyes bright with anticipation.

"He doesn't deserve to be treated like a king," Joyble protested, recalling Stewart's insults.

"Why not, let's show some respect for the position he's held," Elly replied. "I received a call from his replacement, and I understand he'll fly in for the occasion. He's given me an unlimited budget to put the event on, but I can't do it alone. I'll need some help from you gentlemen."

"I'll do the bar," offered Billington, chortling.

"Thanks, Joe," replied Elly, grateful for a positive response, despite the hidden agenda. She waited in silence for a few moments for the others to respond.

"Saturday is always busy on the home front, but I'd be happy to give a short speech," Joyble said at last, as if he were making the contribution of a lifetime.

"The same for me," said Jones unabashedly.

"Thanks a whole lot for nothing, guys. It appears I'll have try to find help elsewhere." Standing up, she turned her back on them and walked over to gaze out the window.

Waiting for them to leave, she couldn't keep her eyes from filling with tears of frustration.

A few minutes passed before she could shake the feeling. She wasn't going to let the men throw a damper on the party. She'd find a way to pull it all together, come hell or high water. There is nothing like non-support to strengthen one's will to succeed, and succeed she would. Without realizing what she was doing, she shouted, "Jerks!"

Rita hurried to Elly's doorway. "I saw the guys come out and then I heard you yell. What have the 'jerks' done now, Elly?"

"You won't believe this! After all Byron has done for those guys—the bonuses he's given them, the drinks on a Friday night, the Christmas dinners—after all that, all those years, they won't lend a hand to put on a retirement party for him."

"You're right—they are jerks," responded Rita. "But never mind, we'll help you. Who needs those jerks, anyway? I'm sure Melody will help. Let's call her in."

"Of course, I'd love to help!" Melody exclaimed, her shrill laughter music to Elly's ears. "I'll help any possible way I can!"

"I'll make floral arrangements for each table," said Rita, beaming with enthusiasm.

"You gals are absolutely great!" Elly said, giving each of them a hug. "This is going to be the best party ever, I just know it. I think I'll invite the whole damn town!"

During the '50s, Sherman's Orchard had been one of the largest in the area—five hundred orange trees, along with two hundred grapefruit and lime trees. Also sharing the rich land two miles north of Summergrove were twenty-five prize quarter horses, complete with a small, recreational riding range. But when the owner passed away, it was bequeathed to the City of Summergrove, which converted into a much-needed park and recreation area. A handful of orange trees remained, and their blossoms filled the air each spring, reminiscent of days gone by.

Summergrove residents were as proud of Sherman's Park as they were of the convention center and the town itself. No one disputed the generous budget needed to keep its flowerbeds tended and to mount the extravagant seasonal decorations. Christmas was exceptionally elaborate, the entire complex a blaze of colored lights, and families came from miles around to see the gigantic Santa and reindeer that appeared to be flying over the roof of the main building.

Approaching the Sherman's Park receptionist, Elly said, "Hello, there! I'm the office manager of Sunshine Linen. I'd like to book the large hall for the general manager's retirement party. I'd like it for May 30—I hope it's free." When the receptionist regretfully informed her all rooms were booked until the end of August, she was demoralized, but determined not to give up.

Early the next morning, while Elly was trying to think of another place that would be large enough, the Sherman's Park receptionist telephoned to notify her there had been a cancellation and the large hall was hers if she still wanted it. "You bet I do!" she responded.

The days flew by, and finally the day of the party arrived. Rita and Melody moved about the hall, attending to last-minute details. A head table for twelve had been prepared for the dignitaries, with Mr. Stewart and wife in the middle, the place of honor. Elly had asked the emcee to place the rest of the dignitaries in the order that would be easiest for making the introductions. Mr. Stewart's replacement, thus far known to Elly only as George Hammerstein transferring in from New York State, would be seated at that table, and Elly was consumed with curiosity to see what he looked like.

A picture of Mr. Stewart and his wife on one of their many trips to Hawaii, Mr. Stewart's favorite, was projected on a large overhead screen where everyone would see it upon entering. The projector would also be used for the main part of the program, a pictorial retrospective of his life.

In collaboration with his wife, Elly had written the story of Mr. Stewart's life and planned to read it as the slides flashed onto the overhead screen. Then they selected relevant pictures from the family album, but could find none from his childhood. So, Elly had substituted a picture of her son Randall at six months old, lying on his stomach, bare-bottomed for the world to see, a big grin on his face. The dimple in his chin could easily pass for Mr. Stewart's cleft—no one would be the wiser. Elly felt delightfully impish, and Mrs. Stewart laughed, "He's going to be blown away when he sees what we have done! We're really giving him a jolly good roasting!"

Gathering at the entrance, Elly and her willing crew stood back and admired the hall. The round tables covered with white linen were centered with mint green squares with matching fan-folded napkins. Rita had made beautiful floral centerpieces of white and cream carnations for each table, and a white card edged with gold presenting the evening's program rested against each wine goblet. "It's simply beautiful!" exclaimed Elly, eyes glistening. "I have been to many events in this hall, but I've never seen this room look as beautiful. Thank you so much, ladies!" Rita and Melody looked at each other and smiled with pride before leaving to check on the bar area.

Elly's thoughts switched back to the new general manager. Just thinking about him made her uneasy. *What if I don't like him? What if he turns out to be an ogre? What if he doesn't like me?* She'd become comfortable with Mr. Stewart and knew his little quirks, and the thought of getting used to someone new was daunting. There was considerable truth in the comment Joyble had made on several occasions: "It's better to have the devil we know than the one we don't."

Her thoughts were interrupted as Rita hurried back and asked, "Shouldn't Joe be here with the bar supplies by now? It's only two hours before the dinner.

"By golly, your right!" exclaimed Elly. "Thanks for thinking of it! Where the heck could he be? I gave him the money. I'd better phone him."

Hurrying out to the phone in the hall, she dialed his pager with a trembling hand. "Where are you, Joe? You should be here by now with the bar supplies," she scolded. "I gave you the money." From the clinking of glasses and roar of conversation in the background, Elly assumed he was in a bar.

"Oh, I guess I didn't tell you—I can't pick up the supplies. I have a lot of other things happening today, other commitments. Sorry. But what money are you talking about, general?"

"You know very well what money!" Elly was almost screaming.

"Just kidding—don't get so excited!" he replied. "It's still in my pocket."

Elly didn't bother to say goodbye and slammed the receiver down so hard she was afraid she'd cracked it. She could feel her anger building as she walked back into the reception room. *How could he let me down like this? Oh, how I hate the drunken sot!* Fortunately, Rita and Melody graciously agreed to go with her to pick up the many cases of beer and other bar supplies.

Rushing to the nearest liquor store, they had the bar set up and ready for the bartender within an hour. However, that left them with less than an hour to go home, get ready, and return for the party. There was no way Elly could get back in time to greet the dignitaries—and get her first look at her new boss.

Although Elly usually liked to take her time getting ready for a party, priding herself on her appearance, she had to settle for a quick shower and a rush job on hair and makeup tonight. She hurriedly slipped into her favorite little black dress, added the expensive single string of pearls Vincent had given her years earlier, put on her best black heels and sped downstairs to join Vincent.

When they arrived at Sherman's Park, the parking lot was filled to capacity, forcing them to hunt for a spot along the road. *That's a good sign*, thought Elly. *It means there's a good turnout!* Preparing an event of this magnitude is a lot of work, but the sea of faces that greeted them as they entered the room made it all worthwhile. It seemed everyone invited came—there were countless guests in the bar area, enjoying conversation and reading the evening's program, while many others had already taken their places at a table. *This is truly a happening!* Elly thought.

Her gaze rested on Joyble and Jones with their wives, dressed to the nines, looking fresh and relaxed, engaged in animated conversation with dignitaries from the head office. Then she spied Billington, seated on a stool at the bar with a drink in his hand, his face flushed and his beaver smile pasted on. He was in his element.

Heading over to tell the emcee that it was time for people to be seated, she passed behind the group of dignitaries, unnoticed by Joyble, and was dismayed to hear him say, "Thanks! Yes, this is a great party and a lot of work. Elly helped me a little."

Swallowing her anger, she continued over to Walter Borski, the route driver who had agreed to be the emcee. He was a jolly person, experienced at public speaking, and Elly knew he would draw chuckles from the audience. Although she had laid out the program in its entirety for him, she'd left areas where he could adlib.

"Walter, I think it's time to have everyone seated. I scheduled the limousine to arrive at the front door at seven fifteen. Everyone in the hall should be seated when the guests of honor enter, to make them more visible. I've asked Rita and Melody to stand and lead the clapping. I know everyone will follow suit."

"Gotcha," said Walter and walked over to the microphone. "Ladies and gentlemen, may I have your attention, please? Tonight is your lucky night! 'Why?' you ask. Allow me to explain. Tonight, the infamous Walter Borski is your master of ceremonies. 'Who is Walter Borski?' you ask. Again, allow me to explain. He's the handsomest, most intelligent man in Summergrove, and you ladies and gentlemen are looking at him!" Everyone laughed and clapped, and the mood was set. He continued, "I understand the evening's celebrities will be here shortly! Please be seated."

Moments later, the limousine pulled up. The Stewarts gasped when they entered the room— not in their wildest imaginations had they expected such a crowd. Mr. Stewart laughed as he pointed at the projector screen and exclaimed to his wife, "Look! It's us in Hawaii!"

"Elly has thought of everything!" Mrs. Stewart said, as Walter escorted them to their place of honor at the head table, accompanied by thunderous applause.

A cornucopia of culinary delights was laid out on three long, skirted tables, a feast for the eyes. Elly had asked the chef to be sure every dish had a garnish. "People eat with their eyes," she'd reminded him. There were platters of all kinds of seafood, an variety of salads centered by an ice swan, a basket of croissants and whole-wheat rolls accompanied by a tub of golden butter, assorted pickles arranged around a turnip "chrysanthemum" and crystal bowls of crispy vegetables in vinaigrette. Buttered vegetables of every kind and color steamed in one chafer, while others held crispy, oven-baked baby potatoes and golden, baked chicken breast. At the end of the line, a large baron of beef, studded with garlic cloves, sat before a chef holding his stance for carving. A separate dessert table held a traditional English trifle topped with whipped cream and cherries, a variety of cheesecakes, fresh fruit compote and a delectable assortment of pastries.

Elly was in the ladies room when the head table was introduced, returning just in time for Joyble's speech. He read from a piece of paper, like an elementary school child, about all the good times he had shared with Stewart, both at and away from work, and how much he would miss him.

Hearing giggling from the tables nearest him, Elly shifted for a better view and saw the reason for their seeming rudeness: Joyble stood there proudly in his fancy evening clothes, hair slicked back and fingernails manicured—completely oblivious to the fact his fly was wide open.

As he returned to his table, his wife whispered something in his ear. And blushing a shade Elly had never seen on a man before, he turned on his heel and scurried for the men's room. *Oh, sweet revenge!* Elly thought.

Next it was Jones's turn to speak. As he passed Elly's chair, he leaned down and whispered, "You're candy for the eyes!"

She shuddered and replied, "Go tell that to your wife."

His tribute to Mr. Stewart was a duplicate of Joyble's. *Doesn't the man have a single original thought in his head?* He did, however, deliver his speech with pizzazz, flashing his white smile at the appropriate pauses and gazing around the room with confidence.

Finally, it was time for Elly to speak. But when she heard Walter call her name, she felt the sudden onset of stage fright, something she never expected. She had been welcoming the chance to express her sentiments to the man who'd hired her when all her chips were down ten years ago, but her legs felt like sticks and her mouth went dry as she walked up to the microphone.

When she began to speak, her voice sounded strange, as if it came from some far corner of the room, "Byron and Sally, honored guests, ladies and gentleman, in 1983 a recession hit Summergrove, the likes of which I hope we never see again." She glanced over to the head table. "When I walked into Sunshine Linen and you hired me—I don't know if you knew it, Byron—I was desperate for the job. So, first, I would like to thank you for having enough faith in me to offer me the position. I will always remember and appreciate it.

"We—and by that, I mean my staff and I—have enjoyed working for you. We have enjoyed your sense of humor, your participation in the office birthday parties, the Christmas socials we've had in the lunchroom. But most of all, Byron, we appreciate the leadership you have given us. You have held this company together during bad economic times and during times when our competitors were trying to sneak into our back door. You have kept everyone gainfully employed, and we thank you for that, too.

"We will miss you very much on the work front, but we don't have to say goodbye. You're staying here in town, and I'm sure we will see you often. Thank you, Byron, for being the greatest boss anyone could ask for. And we hope you and Sally enjoy the years ahead!"

Elly didn't know how she got the words out, but when she'd finished, she received a standing ovation. When she returned to her seat, her eyes wet, Vincent squeezed her trembling hand and exclaimed, "You were great, dear!" *Sweet liar,* she thought.

A few minutes later, composed, she moved to the projector table, as Billington sauntered over, clearly intoxicated. Nonetheless, her fears were allayed when they started with the baby picture to much laughter and applause, setting the lighthearted tone for the rest of the slide show.

When Mr. Stewart approached Elly afterward to thank her for the party, he was accompanied by his replacement. George Hammerstein was six foot five and looked much older than his forty-six years. His angular face held washed-out blue eyes that had an "I'm so smart" look, and his protruding bottom lip did nothing to improve his austere appearance, merely adding an ugly pout. As he walked away after the introduction, Elly noticed the last remnants of his hair clustered at the back of his head and was reminded of the ewok she'd seen in her sons' animal book.

Definitely, better the devil we know than the one we don't! Elly thought despondently.

16

The Devil's Henchmen

George Hammerstein leaned back in his chair, put his hands behind his head, closed his eyes and listened to the hum of activity: people chatting, machines droning beneath his floor and traffic flowing by his window, interspersed by a distant car horn. He'd held his new position as general manager for six weeks now, and each day he'd strolled through the busy plant, visiting each station and engaging the workers in conversation. He never interrupted long for he had to be sure they understood that productivity was important. He'd also held several managers meetings, in the hopes of both building a stronger business and ascertaining who, if anyone, would be his ally. Early on, he knew Eric Joyble was his man.

Leaning forward and glancing toward the office, he turned his thoughts to the women working there. He had a direct view of Anna, Elly's latest recruit, and admired her tall, slim figure. But it was her soft brown eyes and ready smile that pleased him most. She always laughed at his jokes, always brightened his day.

A whole lot more than that sullen Carlita ever does. Strange cookie, that Carlita! But Eric says she's excellent with the customers and does much for the service department. If my favorite and senior manager likes her, it has to count for something.

Above the drone of the machines below, he could hear Melody's laughter in the outer office. He had to admit he liked Melody, so jolly and friendly. He was pleased she'd made friends with his wife, Susan. It helped Susan's self-esteem to have a new friend who was heavier than she was. *We left so many friends behind in New York when we moved to this dumpy one-horse town! I can't figure out why there was so much hype about living in California. Personally, I prefer a four-season climate—I'd take it over the blowing rain any day! Just as soon as I leave my mark here, I'll try for a transfer back.*

He thought about Rita in the computer room. She was definitely a competent, hard worker, but she was distant, more in tune with Elly. They'd barely spoken three words since his arrival. *Doesn't she know I'm in charge?*

Then there was Elly, with her pinched mouth and those buggy eyes that seemed to bore right through him. She was the queen bee of the office and had far too much control, as far as he was concerned. Even when he met with her one on one, she was cool and indifferent. While others laughed at his jokes, she always turned away with her nose in the air. *Who the hell does the redhead think she is? I wish she'd resign—I'd much rather have a younger office manager, anyway, someone like Anna, for example.*

"Elly may be the office manager, but I think I'll also make her my personal secretary. I'll show her who's boss around here!" he murmured. After bouncing the idea around in his head for a few moments, he buzzed her on the phone. "Would you please buy me some lottery tickets, the scratch kind that cost a dollar … and some birthday cards, the generic kind? I plan to give each employee a card and five lottery tickets every time their birthday rolls around.

"I'll need you to give me the birthdates of all the people in the building. No, on second thought, I want you to keep track and remind me when each birthday arises. And keep a good supply of popsicles in the freezer upstairs. I want to give them out to everyone on hot days." He was pleased with himself for thinking of these things. *It's not going to cost much and it will improve my position when it comes to negotiations—well worth it!*

He buzzed Elly again. "And I'd like you to buy some paintings for my office. Get a couple nine by twelves and a larger one, about twenty-four by thirty-six, preferably in oil, preferably water and mountain scenes."

"How much do you want to spend? The scale is quite varied," Elly replied, wondering how long this new task would take.

"Oh, a couple hundred smackeroos should do it."

"I need to finish the daily journals and the inventory count sheets for month end, first, George, but when I'm done, I'll go do it." *Doesn't he know accounting is all consuming at month end? Byron would have been more considerate.* She sighed and kept working on the month-end reports. But every half hour, Hammerstein would ask for the birthday cards, and every half hour she'd answer, "I'm still busy with month end, George."

Although he stopped nagging after a while, Elly couldn't help feeling pressured. And to add insult to injury, during his last call he'd taken it upon himself to remind her to do the managers' payroll, as if Elly would ever forget—after all, she was one of them.

Hammerstein had to admit his dislike for Elly was strictly of a personal nature. He couldn't say one thing against her work habits or loyalty to the company. Her department expenses were always under budget, and Stewart had told him she'd orchestrated a collection method that placed her office top in the country for the lowest percentage of past dues—so important for a successful profit and loss statement at year's end, when the overage versus accrual came directly off the bottom line.

Over the next several months, Hammerstein was quick to learn the full dynamics of his job. He knew the personalities of his managers, their strengths and their weaknesses, and with whom he could form a bond. He also learned how daunting the complexity of the unionized plant workers could be. As in all situations where there is a group of people, there is a hierarchy. This was evident among them, and it didn't take long to realize who carried the weight among the plant workers.

He decided he wouldn't worry about it. He had far more pressing things on his mind, such as the ongoing problem with Billington, whose drinking and money problems were affecting his work. Complaints from his production staff came in each day, and with good reason—Billington was never around when they needed him. These grievances used valuable production time and were piling up, and his department expenses were over budget month after month. *There has to be some way to make a change, to get rid of him!*

It was Friday night and Billington, high on vodka and with an undiluted supply in a large thermos, strolled down to the waterfront. He was in a state of euphoria. He'd picked up some ham ends from the deli on his way home from work—got the works for a buck, a good pound of it—fried them with onion, some leftover spuds and two eggs on top. What a feast it was! And all done in the frying pan Elly had given him.

He tipped back his old blue thermos every so often as he ambled along, savoring the warm feeling the vodka left in his throat. It was a beautiful night. The moon hung low over the water, casting an orange glow. Finding a place to sit in the shadow of a yacht at the end of one of the swaying docks, he twisted his thermos open again and took a long, slow swig. *Ah, nectar of the gods!*

He was running low on money again. It seemed the more he had, the more he needed. And there was no soft touch left at Sunshine Linen anymore. *You'd think that Elly broad with her eagle eyes was the bloody owner, the way she behaves!* He knew he'd have to figure out a new way, but it was like a game he knew he'd win. He always did.

A small sloop pulled into the dark harbor close by. He sat motionless as it putted in slowly and then silently glided up to the dock with the engine cut—he could've reached out and touched it. Two darkly clad men stepped lightly onto the dock, unaware of Billington, who shrank farther into the shadows. A heavily accented voice whispered in the darkness, "Who's de contact? Hurry up! We have to be quick, amigo."

"It's Johnny," replied the other. "De contact's Johnny. Let's unload it and hope like de hell he shows."

Billington's curiosity was piqued as he watched them heave a plastic-wrapped wooden box onto the dock. Imagining the prize that must require this kind of mystery, he snuck through the shadows and approached them from the other side of the dock. Walking quickly toward them, he announced, "Johnny here."

"Here it is," said the stranger. "That'll be fifty grand—cash."

"It was supposed to be forty," said Billington, despite knowing this was no bartering situation. Over the stranger's head, he had seen the watchman's light coming down the dock in their direction—he just needed to stall them for a few more moments. "The agreement was forty," he repeated. When the watchman's light grew close enough that he could almost make out his badge, Billington shouted, "It's the police!"

Without hesitation, the men jumped back into their boat, revved the motor and roared off into the blackness of the sea. It all happened so quickly that Billington, already in a stupor from the many tips of his thermos, hadn't had time to consider his next step. But the watchman's light was drawing closer—he had to think fast!

"What's in the box?" the watchman asked authoritatively.

"Oh, that …" Billington chuckled throatily. "Just some salmon I bought off a fisherman today. It's a heavy son-of-a-gun—I was waiting for some strong guy like you to come along to help me get it to my car."

"I'd be happy to," the watchman agreed, eager for a diversion from the monotony of his job.

Back at his condo, still smiling about how he'd fooled them all, Billington lugged the box into his bedroom. He didn't want his roommates to see it when they got home from the bar. Getting a screwdriver from his nightstand drawer, he stabbed the packaging a few times before finally revealing several hundred small pouches of white powder. It didn't take him long to realize it was cocaine—and an incredible windfall. He instinctively knew there'd be no trouble finding a market. He pushed the box into his closet and threw a blanket over it.

The following Friday, Billington had come in late as usual and sat at his desk wondering how he was going to get through the day. A monster of a headache was pounding behind his eyeballs and his mouth tasted awful, like straw peed on by horses. He was jarred by Hammerstein's loud voice coming over the intercom: "Joe Billington, come to my office." *God, what does he want now?*

"Have a chair," Hammerstein ordered. "I need to have a serious talk with you. For some time now, you've not been meeting the demands of your position. Is there some kind of problem you're having in your personal life you'd like to discuss with me?" He studied Billington's withered face, puffy, yellowish eyes and unkempt appearance, noticing his hands were trembling.

"Problem?" replied Billington, struggling to stuff his hands in his pockets. "Why do you think I'm having a problem? And why do you think I'm not doing my job? The clean loads go out on the drivers' trucks on time, don't they?"

"Yes, the loads go out, but that's more a result of conscientious plant workers who also have a driver on their tail. And that happens long before you show up for work."

"You can't fire me," Billington said smugly. "I'll get a lawyer. It'll cost the corporation one hell of a pile of dough!"

Hammerstein ignored his statements and went on, "Starting Monday, you are relieved of your position as production manager. You will be in charge of linens used in the convention center. You will occupy a desk by the side door. I'll be watching you closely. You must report to me each morning no later than 8:00, at which time I will give you your duties for the day. You have three months to pull up your socks. It's all outlined in this letter."

Billington's usual quick retorts were stuck somewhere in his fuzzy brain. He merely took the letter and walked back to his desk. There, he reflected on the latest turn of events. He, Joe Billington, handpicked by Byron Stewart five years earlier, was now reduced to this. He couldn't remember ever feeling thirstier and buzzed the receptionist, "I have a doctor's appointment—don't expect me back the rest of the day."

With the position of production manager now open, Bert Malestrom, a young driver from Joyble's crews, had asked for an interview.

"Tell me how we'll benefit by hiring you," Hammerstein began.

"For one thing," Malestrom had replied, "I'm more familiar with production than anyone else. For the past few months, I've been doing the morning job—making the loads go out. Billington was never around."

"I've noticed," replied Hammerstein, grinning. "That's why we're talking."

"And one more thing—I am computer literate. As a matter of a fact, there isn't much I don't know about computers. That will come in handy for everyone—I don't believe Elly is too savvy." Malestrom considered himself as a computer whiz—but most of all, he thought of himself as the company's future president, something he wasn't about to tell Hammerstein.

"Well, the job is yours. I'll start training you tomorrow. Here are your benefits, pay and bonus outline." Hammerstein said and handed him a sheet of paper.

Malestrom was thrilled and eager to tell his wife he had started his climb up the corporate ladder. Determined to succeed, he sat proudly in Billington's chair, looking as if he'd always been there. Elly was pleased Billington would no longer have access to corporate funds and was equally pleased with his replacement, whom she'd previously noticed among the eight drivers. He was courteous, well groomed and appeared honest. His demeanor strongly suggested he was destined for higher places.

Billington, devastated, reluctantly took his daily assignments from Hammerstein, consoled only by the fact he was near the side door and could escape for a clandestine meeting with a junky to sell cocaine. Money was no longer an issue. There was a steady flow of the nectar.

But Hammerstein had not completely solved the problems with his management staff. He had no faith in Bob Jones, either. In the six months he had been there, he hadn't seen Jones bring in one substantial sale. *What does the man do with his time?* Reviewing Jones's file, Hammerstein concluded he didn't even sell enough to cover his own wages.

But he knew changing Jones's status would be even harder than it had been with Billington. Next to Joyble, Jones had been with the company the longest. So, when he called Jones into his office for a serious talk, his last words were merely a stern instruction: "Pull up those sales! Hire more salesmen. Just do whatever it takes to bring up the top line."

Little did Hammerstein anticipate the changes Jones's response to his directive, would bring. The man he hired, Johnny Crowfoot, a tall, handsome twenty-six-year-old Native American, full of pep and humor, laughed loudly when he first shook Hammerstein's hand, displaying remarkable white teeth. He also laughed heartily at all of Hammerstein's jokes, and soon was joking around with him on a regular basis. Before long they became personal friends—to the consternation of the other salesmen and managers, not to mention providing fodder for gossip among the plant workers.

Crowfoot also developed a friendship with Melody and would stop to massage her large neck whenever he passed her chair. Elly, noticing this unseemly gesture, gently berated him one day. "Johnny, can I talk to you for a moment, please?" she asked, mustering all the tact she could. "I know you're just being kind when you rub Melody's neck, but if a customer comes in and sees you, it's not appropriate for a business office."

She was astonished when he responded, "I'll speak to George and see what he thinks." Although she never found out if he ever spoke to Hammerstein about it, she was pleased to note that he never rubbed Melody's neck again.

Within a short time, Crowfoot was in dispute with Jones, who felt he was losing control and not receiving the respect he deserved. Crowfoot, on the other hand, was tired of being put on hold or stood up for meetings, a trait of Jones abhorred by everyone who worked with him. The ongoing dispute came to a head one day when Crowfoot threatened to quit if Jones continued as his immediate boss.

Coupled with complaints from the other salesmen and Jones's low sales the past few months, it was just the impetus Hammerstein needed to make some changes. So, after over twenty years as sales manager, Bob Jones, like Billington, received a demotion.

Beginning to feel threatened, Joyble felt a need to speak with Elly. He complained, "I wonder who'll be next, you or I? I've noticed George doesn't like the older staff. He's all for the young. It's absolutely disgusting how he pals around with Johnny like they were brothers or something. It's not proper to socialize with a subordinate. I hear when Johnny got married last summer in San Diego, George was his best man. Can you believe it? And just recently he was also the godfather to his baby!"

Elly found it hard to have compassion for either Billington or Jones. In her mind, both had become complacent and didn't deserve the positions they'd held for so long. She felt the same about Joyble, but she could see he was truly worried and did feel sorry for him. He'd recently had a serious falling out with two of his daughters, and now they'd have nothing to do with him. She remembered when he and his wife had declared at her first staff Christmas dinner that their grown children were not welcome to visit them overnight. *How sad!*

Pushing those thoughts aside, she responded, "We can only do our best with our jobs on a day-by-day basis, Eric. No one can ask any more from us. I agree George is breaking all the rules known to business, and his relationship with Johnny could very well backfire one of these days."

Elly could not figure out what was happening with Hammerstein. He had isolated himself from the staff, spending hours on the phone with his door closed, questions pertinent to the accounting function and the results of the bottom line left unanswered. And he was out of the office for hours at a time.

Less and less was being seen of Crowfoot, too. But when he did arrive on the scene, he could be heard all over the plant as he shouted greetings to the workers.

"Keep up the good work, ladies! I'm proud of you!" he'd yell as he walked through the plant. However, his sales, which were quite impressive at the start, had dropped off alarmingly.

17

Flattery's Double Edge

It was toward the end of summer, Hammerstein called all the staff together in the boardroom: Elly, Rita, Melody, Anna and Carlita from the office, along with Joyble, Jones, Billington and a couple of the other sales staff. Crowfoot also was there, center stage, wearing an uncharacteristic frown.

Elly pondered the purpose of the meeting. *Did the company decide to sell the business? Is George leaving to go somewhere else? And why is Johnny looking so downtrodden?*

After everyone settled into the room, Hammerstein said in a dramatic voice, "I've called you here today because Johnny has an announcement. The floor is all yours, Johnny."

All eyes turned to Crowfoot, who, to everyone's horror, began to cry. With tears streaming down his face, he finally choked out, "I'm a cocaine addict and have been for some time. I'm going to try to shake it. I'm going into rehab. George said the company would pay for it." With that, he began sobbing so hard, he couldn't go on.

Everyone was shocked. The ladies, overcome with sympathy, also had tears running down their faces. The men looked stunned and much less sympathetic. Through her own tears, Elly studied Hammerstein. He had a strange look in his eyes, as if he were enjoying the drama. *Whatever possessed him to have Johnny confess in front of everyone? Was it part of the treatment process or just a self-glorifying act to make everyone think of him as the good guy, the savior?*

She scolded herself for the negative thoughts—after all, helping anyone from the scourge of addiction was noble in itself. Looking at Billington and noticing his yellowish skin and blood-shot eyes, she couldn't help wondering why *he* wasn't given the same chance for rehabilitation. *Was it because he was older and considered less deserving? Or was it because he hadn't become George's personal friend?*

After shaking Crowfoot's hand and wishing him well, everyone dazedly returned to their desks, emotionally drained and unable to concentrate on their work the rest of the afternoon. Billington went home early again, now deeply troubled about the contents of his closet. He'd finally put two and two together about the dockside strangers' contact. *How stupid of me! The cocaine was meant for Crowfoot—he's been selling the stuff!*

The next morning, Billington arrived at the office unusually early. He hadn't felt like drinking the night before—which was unusual, too. He couldn't erase the sight of a young man like Crowfoot breaking down and crying like that in front of everyone. *And all because of drugs!* He slipped into his side door and sat quietly at his desk, pondering his life. He thought about all the money he'd wasted, all the money he'd stolen and all the people he'd hurt, especially his family, the grown daughter he didn't know and the young son whose mother he'd married only for the child's sake. Taking the Yellow Pages from his desk drawer, he flipped to the listing of churches, made a selection and dialed the number. "Hello. Are you a priest?" His heart was beating fast and he'd broken a sweat. He couldn't believe he was actually doing this or that he was so nervous about it.

"Yes, Father Mulligan here, rector of St. Francis of Assisi . Can I help you, brother?"

"I need to talk to you. I need to talk to you badly," Billington blurted.

Hearing the desperation and edgy hoarseness in Billington's voice, the young priest assumed it was an alcohol-related problem, his second that week. "I have an hour and a half before mass starts and a funeral directly after. Can you drop by right now?" asked the priest.

"Yes, oh, yes," Billington agreed. "Where can I meet you?"

"Lets meet at the cathedral," replied the priest in a gentle voice. "It's peaceful and quiet there."

"Is that the church on the hill, south of town, with a statue of a monk in front?"

"Yes, that's right," replied the priest. "That monk is St. Francis… I'll wait there for you, near the statue—it's a beautiful morning."

"I'll be right there!"

The words fell out of his mouth in a raspy stream as he told his life story to the priest, confessions of alcohol abuse, petty thievery, betrayals, cocaine and, finally, Crowfoot. "How do I make it right? How do I change?" His yellowed eyes pleaded earnestly.

"You're already in the process of changing, just by being here. Sometimes, you have to hit rock bottom before you really change. You must join Alcoholics Anonymous—they'll help you immensely. Then you must follow the law of the land. Return everything you've stolen—but first and foremost, it's imperative you tell the police what happened on the dock and hand over the cocaine. If you like, I'll accompany you and speak on your behalf and plead for leniency. Finally, I think it would be helpful if you moved your family to a new town, where you can start a new life. You can contact me anytime if you feel it's necessary to talk further. And remember, son, we do not walk alone in this life. The Lord will walk with you, if you welcome him."

When he returned to his office, Billington contemplated the priest's words, but the thought of existing without alcohol seemed unbearable, like living in the desert without water. *I'll have to think about this for a while. Perhaps tomorrow or next week, I'll turn over a new leaf—at the very latest, next month. I can't think about it right now.* He mumbled an expletive and reached for his flask.

An unshakeable pall had fallen over the office after Crowfoot's confession. The administrative staff worked in morose silence, and every time Elly closed her eyes, she saw his crying face. She wondered if he would be successful in beating the drug scourge, knowing the odds were against him. She also wondered about Billington and Jones. *Will another letter be coming from George with more staff changes?*

A staff change came, all right—with a lot more ferocity than a letter. A police car sitting in the middle of the parking lot when Elly returned from lunch forced her to drive around to get to her designated spot. As she stepped out of her car, she heard a man's raspy voice screaming pitifully, "Let me go! Let me go! I didn't do anything! I'm innocent! I'm one of the managers here!"

"Oh, my God, it's Joe!" Elly declared, recognizing him bent over the back of the police car, his face pressed against the trunk, as two police officers struggled to handcuff him. The color drained from her face as she watched the dehumanizing episode in horror.

"You're under arrest for trafficking in cocaine. You have the right to remain silent. And you have the right to counsel. If you do not have one, the court will appoint one for you." The words seemed to bounce off the steam tunnel at the side of the building. And within seconds, the parking lot was full of inquisitive employees, drawn by the commotion.

Intermittent gasps came from the crowd as Billington fought off the policemen's efforts to subdue him. Although he was strong as a bull, the police were finally able to force him into the back seat of the police car, but he kept kicking so they couldn't shut the door. They struggled for several minutes to control him, but it was futile—his soccer training had built strong leg muscles. They needed more help, and one of the policemen radioed for assistance.

Within seconds, two more policemen arrived on the scene, making a total of six. It took all of them to pull Billington from the back seat and get him on the ground. Elly heard the thud when he hit, but he kept right on fighting. His voice, now only a whisper, could barely be heard above the orders of the police. They hog-tied him, thrust him onto the back seat and closed the door.

In the alcoholic fuzziness of his tortured mind, Billington suddenly understood the meaning of rock bottom when he heard cheers and hoots rising from the crowd. They had not been so ful-ly entertained since Melody danced with that pinned-on append-age at the Christmas dinner. But what Billington didn't know would have given him cause to thank the policemen. He didn't know the undercover cop who'd initiated his arrest had saved him from certain death. As crafty as he'd become, he'd stepped into a whole new territory when he took up the drug trade. There was a price on his head for selling merchandise belonging to the cartel.

"Whatever will happen to his family, his wife, his child?" Elly's rhetorical question reached the ears of an employee standing nearby.

"Oh, I've heard he doesn't live with his wife and child. Hasn't for months—probably never did.

Elly watched the police car disappear around the corner and was filled with a type of sadness she'd never experienced. *To see a human so degenerated all because of alcohol. What power to destroy it has!* Yet, she also felt relief that Billington was gone. It would greatly simplify her role as "protector of corporate funds."

Hammerstein had been enjoying a long lunch break that day and missed the donnybrook. When Elly told him, the muscles in his face relaxed and he made only one comment, "Finally, that's the end of that!"

Hardly a day passed that Hammerstein didn't mention how well Crowfoot was doing with rehab. "You wouldn't know it was the same man," he'd commented to Elly. "He's an altogether dif-ferent person. He's quiet now and anxious to come back to work and dig his heels in. I've visited him every day and I've seen a re-markable improvement each time I go."

Two weeks later, Crowfoot returned, fresh and bright-eyed, and surprisingly quiet. But Joyble was concerned and went in to chat with Elly, something he was doing more frequently lately. "This drug thing isn't easily cured. We'll have to watch him carefully."

"I'm sure it must be a difficult thing to overcome," replied Elly. She thought of her sons, now practicing medicine in Oregon, and felt eternally grateful.

"Johnny may appear cured now, but it's far too soon to shout victory. The question is what he will be like a year from now, two years from now," Joyble declared.

Hammerstein, however, had a lot more confidence in Crowfoot. He promoted him to manager of a sub-office he'd opened in a middle-sized town sixty miles northwest of Summergrove. As astounded as the staff had been by Crowfoot's drug confession, it paled in comparison to the hubbub his promotion caused. The shocking news buzzed around the plant.

But other things were now giving Elly concern. Carlita had become even more uncooperative and sullen, verbalizing her complaints about every little annoyance. Her noise and bluster were getting on the nerves of her co-workers, especially Anna, whose desk was five feet away. "I don't think I can take much more of her. I start to calculate payroll and she distracts me. I no sooner start something else and she tells me to go for coffee. She is continually interrupting me and bossing me around!"

"Have you spoken with her about how you feel, Anna? Sometimes, it only takes a little gentle conversation painted with a smile."

"I've tried. She's OK for a few days, and then she starts it all over again. If she doesn't stop immediately, I'm going to have to look for another job—or lose my sanity."

"Please, Anna, don't do anything impulsive. You're appreciated around here. I'll keep an eye on her, Anna, and when I notice something amiss, I'll call her in for a talk. Don't let her be the reason you give up your position—she's not worth the loss. Let's give it a week and see what happens. She won't need to know you've spoken to me."

Shortly after Anna's visit, Elly witnessed a performance by Carlita that was the last straw. In a fit of rage, Carlita had sworn aloud and given the photocopier a resounding kick because it ran out of paper, the commotion distracting everyone from their work once again. Elly immediately buzzed Joyble, who luckily was in his office. "Can you come and see me for a moment, please? I have something very important to discuss with you."

"Sure," replied Joyble, laying down his newspaper. "I can spare a few moments."

"You must have heard the disturbance Carlita made a few seconds ago?"

"Come to think of it, maybe I did hear something. Did a chair fall over?"

"No, it was Carlita kicking the sam hell out of the photocopier," replied Elly, knowing he was fully aware. She continued, "As one manager to another, I need to ask for your support. I have to discipline Carlita today—I have no choice in the matter. She's misbehaving and having temper tantrums, and her behavior is causing a lot of problems for the office, not to mention if it should happen in the presence of a customer. Anna has threatened to quit because of it, and I'd sure hate to lose her. She works extremely hard and is diligent in everything she does."

Pausing, Elly searched for words of diplomacy, but instead fell back on her old friend, Mr. Flattery. "You have always been excellent with the staff, Eric. And I think the service you give our customers is superlative. I know you wouldn't want any of them witnessing this behavior should they be in the office."

Joyble flushed and said, "Of course, I realize you have to reprimand her. You're her supervisor. I can assure you, I would do the same if one of my drivers were misbehaving that way." Standing up abruptly, he turned on his heel and left. Elly knew she did not have his cooperation. "Thanks, Eric! I knew I could count on you!" she called out in a sweet voice just before he closed his door with a bang, intended or otherwise.

Then, she called Carlita into her office. "Your behavior, Carlita, is totally unacceptable. Everyone heard your outburst a few minutes ago. I'm just happy there were no customers in the office for your little performance. Why do you behave like that? Is there something I can help you with?"

Carlita immediately started to cry. "My job is very hard, you know. There is so much distraction all around me, I find it hard to concentrate. And I have so much work to do, I don't know where to start."

"None of those things justify your behavior, Carlita. I want you to go back to your desk and work quietly. And I mean quietly! If there are any more outbursts, I'm going to have to suspend you for several days without pay, and you don't want that happening. I'm sorry, but you leave me no choice."

"I'll try to improve," Carlita said, hanging her head.

Following their talk, Carlita fell into a pout, and a quiet serenity settled the office for the rest of the afternoon. Anna was pleased Elly was finally dealing with the Carlita problem, but although Carlita was a problem, Elly felt compassion for her. At thirty-five, she was unmarried, living alone with her cats, and seemed to lead an unhappy life, that unhappiness undoubtedly affecting her work.

At the end of the day, however, Elly was disgusted to see the large-print letter posted on the bulletin board for all employees to read:

On behalf of the corporation, I would like to compliment Carlita Madsen on the fine job she is doing! Many customers have told me how nice she is on the phone and when they visit the office. This company is very lucky indeed to have her as an employee.

Signed Eric Joyble

Service Manager, Sunshine Linen

Once again, Joyble had undermined her authority and put her in a ridiculous position. He had prevented her from adequately dealing with Suzie, and now he was doing the same thing with Carlita. Clearly, he held all the aces, using his light-hearted, friendly attitude and overstated support at management meetings to ingratiate himself with both Stewart and Hammerstein. To further enhance his position, whenever he re-signed a large contract, he'd announce that he'd saved another account—even though the customer had never even thought about going elsewhere.

It didn't take long for the same old problems with Carlita to resurface. Pondering this dilemma, Elly decided to move her from the middle of the room into a small office where the file cabinets were stored. This would allow peace and quiet for the other ladies in the office and protect the good name of Sunshine if a customer were in the office during one of Carlita's outbursts. Unfortunately, it also gave her the prestige of having her own office, which she attributed to the letter Joyble had posted. Soon, she'd adopted a superior attitude toward everyone, except Joyble, of course. That was exactly how he wanted it.

A few weeks later, Hammerstein was so pleased with all the good work Joyble seemed to be doing, he announced he was going to hire someone as his assistant. He wanted Joyble to spend all his time saving the large accounts, since his past efforts had been so effective. A bulletin posted on the lunchroom wall for all union members to read advertised the assistant service manager position. Several drivers, eager to be part of the management team and knowing they could handle the duties of the advertised position with ease, applied.

As Elly approached the main office after lunch one afternoon, Rita motioned through the computer room window for her to come in. "I heard something incredible in the lunchroom," she said under her breath. "Eric told Carlita to apply for the assistant service manager job, and she thinks she's got it in the bag!"

"No!" gasped Elly. "I don't believe it! She has to be able deal with customer complaints, make route changes and even drive a truck sometimes. She's just not qualified."

"It's as true as I'm sitting here," said Rita. "He all but promised her the job. But George has the last say, doesn't he?"

"He certainly does," responded Elly, wondering why on earth Joyble led Carlita to believe she had a chance.

When the day came for Hammerstein to announce his selection, all hell broke loose in the office. Walter Borski, the jolly man who'd been the master of ceremonies at Mr. Stewart's farewell party, was the lucky competitor. He was very happy, and Elly was delighted, believing he was the most deserving. But Carlita stalked into her office, slamming the door so hard a picture fell off the wall, and threw an absolute tantrum. The office staff could hear her swearing and throwing things around.

Suddenly, all went silent. Worried about Carlita's personal safety, Elly slowly opened the door. The office was a shambles, and Carlita was slumped at her desk, sobbing uncontrollably, her face buried in her arms. Intending to offer comfort, Elly put her arm around Carlita. But before she could speak, Carlita flung her arm back and hit her in the shoulder, nearly knocking her to the floor. "Get the hell out of here!" she screamed.

Elly did just that and vowed never to approach her again. *Fate will take care of things—it always does.* Her sore shoulder bothered her for days, but it couldn't compare to the sick feeling she had about Joyble. He was accustomed to using others for his own selfish purposes, but this time he had given false hope to a woman who clearly needed psychiatric help.

On the other hand, the experience gave Carlita a new mission. She offered herself for the shop steward position now available. Almost every day during the next few months, she left the office for a union meeting. If there weren't any grievances, she'd try to create some. *I'll get even with this damn company one way or the other!*

While Carlita was plotting behind her closed door, a revolutionary new technology was introduced in the office—the Internet. Everyone in the office realized it was a great invention, placing the company in direct communication with the head office and allowing customers to place orders by e-mail, but the full impact of its capabilities became known only as time went on.

"So many changes have happened these past fifteen years I've been with Sunshine!" Elly commented to her staff. "One thing is certain—change will always be with us. Nothing remains the same forever, and we must learn to flow with its tide."

Rita said, "You're darn right! We have to stay with it." Anna and Melody agreed, but Carlita, standing at the photocopy machine, said nothing.

Carlita had other things on her mind, such as the telephone conversations she'd been having with the shop steward at a sister convention center about the renewal of the labor contract. *All this babbling about change from the Internet is nuts. I'll show Elly what real change is all about!*

If Elly thought Hammerstein had been acting strangely before calling that infamous meeting for Crowfoot's confession, her estimation was soon surpassed. He'd become remote and indifferent toward her, demanding, yet incommunicative most of the time. He spent hour after hour on the phone with his door shut. When it was open, he spoke in hushed tones. In one of her private meetings with Rita, Elly noted, "There's something in the wind. I can feel it in my bones. Everything is weird around the office."

When Hammerstein decided to buy new computers for the office, instead of having Elly coordinate them, he assigned Bert Malestrom, the new production manager. He didn't even give Elly the courtesy of explaining why he overstepped protocol. It was a slap in her face.

Bert obviously was embarrassed by the assignment. "Sorry, Elly," he said, as he moved around the office, screwdriver in hand. He brought an old computer in for Elly to use, and then installed brand-new ones for Hammerstein and himself.

The joy of everyday work was fading fast, the turmoil since Hammerstein's arrival unending. For the first time, Elly was finding life within the office difficult. When she left work that day, she decided she needed to talk to Vincent about her change in attitude.

She found him at the far end of their backyard, with a man from the local nursery, standing knee-deep in a trench they'd dug, a dozen little trees nearby ready for planting. As she approached, she instantly identified the trees. "Orange trees, how very thoughtful of you!" He knew she loved the perfume of their blossoms. She glanced at him and returned his smile.

Later, when they were having tea, Elly said, "You know, I think I want to retire. Do you think I should?" Vincent, who had retired four years earlier, was waiting for those very words. "I think you should go for it! We'll finally be able to spend time together." As he gazed into her eyes, the years peeled back, and he saw the beautiful girl he'd made a date with at the military station and longed to have at his side twenty-four seven.

"I'll see how I feel by the end of June 2001. It would be wonderful to have a summer to myself. I want to plant all kinds of flowers, especially dahlias. I saw some in someone's yard last summer as big as dinner plates."

Elly was quiet for a while, listening to the warbling of the sparrows high in the cherry tree, then continued, "You know, dear, I've never really had a decent vacation. I could only take ten days at a time, and those had to be in the middle of the month, so I'd be back for month-end tasks. And even then, the company wouldn't replace me while I was gone, and I'd have to work twice as hard when I returned. It sure would be nice to have free time, after all these years. Maybe we could take a nice long cruise. I'd love to see Alaska."

"I'd love that, too, hon," Vincent agreed. "And when we return, I'd love to get a little pooch—not a big dog, just a little pooch."

18

The Axe Falls

Again, as every year, Elly prepared her Christmas roast beef dinner for the staff. With rain pelting down and the hood on her trench coat pulled up high over her head, she was bent over the trunk of her car, organizing the chafing dishes to take home, when Rita walked by. "Great food, Elly," she said.

"Why thank you, Rita! Say, have you seen Sammy lately? I usually see him at the corner. Today, he's nowhere in sight. I hope he's not sick or injured. I wanted to give me some roast beef."

"Oh, I doubt he's sick. He probably moved to another location. Vendors often do that, especially if business drops off. I haven't seen him for a few days, either"

The next morning, December 22, 1999, as she was leaving for the office, Elly noticed a letter on the hallway table. The return address was O'Malley, Shawnigan and Blynne, Attorneys at Law. Puzzled, she tucked it into her purse. "If it were really important, they'd call," she thought aloud.

Her mind was soon occupied by more pressing issues. The entire world was buzzing with warnings that all computers would crash when the new century arrived. Letters of concern were coming in from suppliers and customers alike. Elly responded to all with a form letter assuring that Sunshine was well prepared for the new millennium. While the letters didn't stop, the rain did, just long enough for the sun to poke out as Elly parked her car.

Hurrying to the front door, she inadvertently stepped in a puddle. The squishing of the wet shoe brought a vivid memory of her first day at Sunshine, when she'd done exactly the same thing. In her office, trying to dry out her shoe, she noticed all the other managers go into Hammerstein's office and thought it was odd she wasn't asked to join them.

At last, George buzzed her just as the others were leaving. "Can you please come in for a minute, Elly?" he said, his voice mysteriously low.

Something's strange here, she thought. *He actually said please!* He sat behind his desk with a sheaf of papers in front of him and the same gleam in his eye she'd noticed when Crowfoot delivered his infamous speech about being an addict. "An important memorandum has come in from head office, and I have instructions to pass its information on to you and your staff. I have already discussed this with the other managers."

Elly sat motionless, waiting for him to continue, her gigantic eyes open to their fullest.

"I have some disturbing news and might as well get right to the point." His voice was deeper than usual and he spoke in a slow monotone, as though he'd been practicing. "Corporate headquarters has decided to centralize the entire accounting function to San Diego." Before Elly could digest what he had said, he continued, "You are probably asking why, and I'll answer that for you. It's because of the demands our sister companies have been placing on equality of wages."

Quickly, Elly asked, "Does that mean my staff will lose their jobs?"

"Rita, as senior, will be the one that will remain," he responded. "We are compelled to keep one union person."

Thank God for that!

A myriad of reasons why moving the accounts was not a good idea crowded her mind, but before she could voice them, Hammerstein spoke again, as though he could read her mind. "The decision to do this has been made and is not open to discussion."

"Does this mean I'll lose *my* job?" she asked, her unwavering eyes studying his face intently.

"Yes and no," he said. "Yes, the job you have today will be gone. But you can transfer to another branch, if you so choose. Or you could go out on the road and do service work for our customers."

Before Elly could respond, he stood up with his arms outstretched to give her a hug and said, "I'm sorry."

But the gleam in his watery eyes told her he wasn't the least bit sorry, and she dodged his approach. *Damned if I'll let him hug me! I don't need consoling.* In fact, she didn't care one iota about losing her job. Instead, she marveled at the irony of the news coming on the heels of her conversation with Vincent about retiring.

"I want you to assemble all of your staff in the boardroom so I can explain it to them," he said. "Let's do it immediately and get this bad news over with."

Elly returned to the office and asked the girls to go into the boardroom. She whispered to Rita, "This is the big one. It explains why things have been so weird around here lately." As they all sat around the table in the boardroom, Elly could see horror on their faces as Hammerstein explained the corporate decision and that they could transfer into the plant to do manual labor if they so chose. As sad as she was for the others, Elly just couldn't feel sorry for Carlita, who sat silently with a scowl frozen on her countenance.

When the meeting was over and Hammerstein had departed, Elly requested her staff to stay for a few moments. "I want you to know I will do my utmost to help you secure another job, when the time comes. There's one thing I would ask of you, though, and I know it will be difficult. I want you to keep your spirits up and try to do the best job you can, right up to the end. I know that is a lot to ask of you right now, but I know you will feel better for it. We are approaching our corporate year-end, and I would like to see us collect all the outstanding accounts we can. Let's hold our heads high and be the best in the corporation once again—not because of this bad news, but in spite of it."

Everyone but Carlita agreed. She had stomped out before Elly finished speaking.

It was late spring 2000 and all signs pointed to a hot summer ahead. A peacock-blue sky surrounded a sun so bright it made Elly squint as she walked across her back yard to check the orange trees before driving to work downtown. She was pleased to see they were well rooted and healthy-looking.

At the office, Rita handed her the age listing of the past due accounts. She had torn the perforated pages apart and divided them among Melody, Anna and herself. Carlita had refused to help phone the customers, stating she had far too much other work to do. Walking in just in time to hear her flat refusal, Elly had responded, "Carlita, you will be responsible for answering the calls that come in while the rest of us are phoning."

The staff began their telephone quest to collect the outstanding accounts in earnest, making one call after the other, nonstop. Elly had told them not to be buffaloed by the old "It's in the mail." She also reiterated the importance of being courteous but forthright when asking the customers for money. "It doesn't hurt one bit to tell them we're striving to be the best within the corporation once again. People like to help winners stay winners."

Sometimes they drove their cars to pick up checks others were delivered by couriers, picked up by route drivers and, in some cases, hand-delivered by the customer. Elly began faxing thank-you letters to the larger companies as the payments rolled in. Finally, when month end came and the last check was posted in the computer against the accounts receivable, they had achieved a full percentage point better than the previous year, a record for the collection of past dues within the entire corporation.

Elly thought she would burst with pride! These ladies who were about to lose their jobs still had the inner fortitude to face adversity head on. Their extraordinary efforts saved the company bad debt expense, thereby increasing year-end profit, and Hammerstein was pleased—he would ultimately reap the benefits. But Elly knew the staff was unaware of this fact—they had labored because of her and her alone. Of course, Carlita was the exception. She had plans of her own, but it would be midsummer before her plans were known.

Meanwhile, Hammerstein and Maelstrom spent hours mulling over the clauses of the union contract, which would expire in seven days, scrambling to submit a new proposal. And just as in other years when contract renewal was drawing near, there was a slowdown of productivity and a buzz of unrest among the workers.

Finally, they believed they had a proposal that would start the negotiations. Hammerstein cunningly had taken from one area, added to another and tossed in a small perk to make it appear the employees were benefiting. Apparently, he didn't realize the paycheck rules supreme. Nor did he realize the potential ramifications.

The union negotiators took one look at his proposal and shot it down. The workers wanted more money, plain and simple, a whole lot more money—certainly a lot more than a birthday card and lottery ticket and a popsicle on a hot summer day. The union walked out of negotiations.

A stumbling block for the corporation was a sister plant that had received a 25 percent increase the year before and now was asking for another increase. It was only natural for Sunshine workers to demand parity. But they also had to realize their demands were exorbitant and could literally close the plant down.

"The buggers are having a strike vote next Monday," Hammerstein declared at the managers meeting. With his bottom lip protruding like a child in pout, he continued, "If they go out on strike, we'll be in big trouble. Our competitors with non-union workers will undercut us as sure as I'm sitting here. They're waiting at the door like hungry wolves as we speak, waiting to snatch all the customers they can. We may even have to close our doors."

Carlita, now shop steward, spent her days visiting every employee in the plant, weaving her web of discontent. She was going to get even with the company if it was the last thing she did on the face of this earth! She encouraged everyone to vote yes to the strike, "If the company knows we mean business about striking, they'll cave in and pay us more. They can't afford to be closed, not even for a day. You'll end up with more money in your pocket."

On the day of the vote, Carlita stood at the bottom of the stairs, smiling at each employee as they headed up to the lunchroom to cast their votes. When the count was complete, the result was nearly unanimous. Everyone had voted to strike, except one person.

Enraged, Hammerstein summoned all his managers into his office. "How can they do that to me after all I've done for them? After giving them lavish Christmas parties and birthday cards with lottery tickets, how can they do this to me?" He buried his face in his hands, and Elly worried he may be having a nervous breakdown. "Now we could arrive to work one morning and find them picketing. But I really don't believe they will actually do it. Too many of them are the only breadwinners in their families. They simply can't afford to be without a paycheck." Hammerstein looked around the room for his staff's reactions.

"I'll bet my grandfather's farm, Rita was the one that voted, no," declared Elly, although she would never ask her.

While everyone was preparing to go home for the weekend, Joyble hung back to have a chat with Elly. "I don't know if George informed you or not, but I'm going to be away on vacation starting Monday," he said, "away for six long weeks."

Elly gulped at the duration but didn't allow her resentment to show. She retrieved her payroll calendar from her drawer to mark in the days. "No, as a matter of fact, he didn't tell me—probably totally slipped his mind. And no wonder, he's had a tremendous amount to contend with these days, what with negotiations and now an affirmative strike vote."

A week later, in the dead heat of August, Elly received a call from Hammerstein at her home at six o'clock in the morning. He was breathless and she could barely hear him. "The employees are on strike! There's a picket line in front of the building as we speak, and it's crucifying business for the convention center. I've already had a call from the manager. Our courier phoned me at home early this morning, thank goodness, or we wouldn't have known.

"You are to drive to my house and leave your car here. We all are going to wear casual clothes, jeans, track shoes, etc., and walk across the picket line together, as a group, to show our strength. They think they are surprising us, but they aren't. We're having the last laugh. Be at my house at 6:45 A.M. sharp!"

When Elly arrived at Hammerstein's house, all the other managers and salesmen were there, except Joyble, who was on his six-week vacation. Carlita was on vacation, too, so would not lose any pay. *How convenient for both of them!* Jones, Elly and Billington's replacement got in the back seat of Hammerstein's car for the ride downtown. Jones said, "Ha, I have always wanted to get Elly in the back seat of a car!"

"Smarten up, Bob, you old flirt," she responded. "You're too old to be fantasizing about such nonsense!" The others laughed.

There were three carloads headed for the Convention Center, with ten men and one woman. All were to park in a selected area across the street. As they approached the front of the building, they could see the picket line snaking along the sidewalk, back and forth, back and forth. Out in front, looking very much like a Sergeant Major, was Carlita, having the vacation of her life! Her face flushed and eyes glistening with excitement, she shouted orders that could be heard for blocks, "Keep the line moving!"

The picketers made a few disgruntled jeers at the management team as they walked past and entered the building. Once inside the safe haven of the building, Hammerstein told them his plan. "We need to get as much as possible counted in and washed before the soiled garments are destroyed by rot. We have four days to accomplish our task, after that rot will set in. We have enough packing slips to send out a few trucks today. We'll do it in the evening after everyone has gone home. Let's try to keep this plant running at least 50 percent capacity. I've no idea how long it's going to last, but we just can't knuckle under to their high demands. I have the different jobs in the plant divided as follows: Bert loading the washers, salesmen operating the flat iron and folding, Bob and Elly counting in the dirty."

Elly was horrified. She remembered what the lady that worked at that station had said one day when she'd met her in the bathroom. Elly had asked how things were going and she'd said, "Fine, if it weren't for the maggots." Elly never forgot it. Contemplating what was ahead with immense apprehension, she mustered up her fortitude. *I can wear a mask, rubber gloves and a big apron and just pretend it's flowers I'm counting,* she told herself. Sales manager Bob Jones and office manager Elly Thomas walked through the dirty plant to take up their new duties at the count-in table.

Hammerstein has done this to make me quit, and if I do that, he won't have to pay severance when the accounts are transferred. I'll show him!

Everything was a mess. Whoever worked the Friday before would have known about the strike and had purposely left unfinished work behind. The floor had not been swept and was littered with the dredge from the laundry bags—scrunched paper napkins, food particles, bits of string, cigarette butts, ashes and old wrinkled soil-tickets. Full and half-empty boxes of bathroom products filed an entire corner of the main floor. The overhead assembly line of bags filled with soiled linen reminded Elly of rotting sides of beef hanging in a broken-down cooler, the smell so vile one hated to breath.

In addition to the table linen from the restaurants, there was the oily smell of coveralls from the automotive repair shops, but worst of all, by far, were the hand towels and aprons that came from the meat distribution places. Writhing maggots crept out from under everything she touched. She shuddered, as did Bob Jones on the other side of the table. What an abhorrent, disgusting, nasty job! But with as much inner strength as she could muster, she put mind over matter and kept right on emptying the bags and counting the items before tossing them into the shoots through the hole in the floor and into the washing machines below.

Each day, they worked long and hard and managed to fill several small trucks at the rear of the building for a fast after-dark delivery to the main customers. They talked about the strike and its ramifications during their coffee breaks, while listening through the open window to Carlita's twangy voice telling the picketers to keep the line moving. And each time they heard her, the men would say, "There goes that witch again, that witch with a capital B!"

While the picket line kept moving up and down the street, the public, most of whom were unionized workers from the local mill, would toot their horns in approval as they drove by. Carlita had thought of everything. When the workers were preparing for a strike vote, she used her guise as shop steward to influence their decisions while making her rounds, knowing full well that she would be on vacation, collecting pay during this period. She would show this company what power she had. She'd fix them for *not* giving her the service assistant job, and she wasn't about to lose any pay in the process.

Glancing through the plant window as she walked by with the strikers, Rita caught a glimpse of Elly working at the putrid counting table. *Wouldn't you know it! They've put Elly on the dirtiest job of all. She should be folding the towels!* Filled with despair, she walked on with her head down, thinking *Damn that Hammerstein! He should know better than to put a senior employee on a job like that. He needs a swift kick in the old wazoo, and I'd love to be the one to give it to him.*

On the morning of the fifteenth day, Bob Jones hurried directly over to Elly, who had beaten him to the count-in table. "You better go outside quickly! It looks like one of the drivers is giving your Vincent a bad time. I could hear Vincent saying something about a key."

"Oh, my God! I forgot to leave the key for him, and he couldn't get into the house. Darn! How can I be so forgetful?" lamented Elly. She undid her apron and went outside. As she faced all the workers on the picket line, she could hear one of the drivers accusing Vincent of trying to sneak into work. It was the one driver known as a hothead and a bully. She handed Vincent the key to the house and then said to the driver, "Please don't be disrespectful to my husband."

The driver charged toward her, saying, "Are you threatening me? Are you threatening me?" Elly put her hand up and the tip of her finger touched the pocket on his shirt sending him into a shouting rage. "I've been struck in the chest by management! I've been struck in the chest by management!"

The strikers, distracted by his shout gathered around him, until they heard Carlita barking her famous orders - "Keep the line moving!" At this point, out of the corner of her eye, Elly saw Vincent feign a punch. This was immediately followed by a blow from the bully, but Vincent was ready for it and ducked. Instead, the driver's fist hit the doorframe of Vincent's car. He quickly left wincing all the way to his truck.

The next day, Elly noticed the bully had a cast on his hand. The incident became the talk of the strike among workers and managers alike. The managers kidded her, saying Vincent and she were "The Dueling Barracudas." They also had a new admiration for Elly. Despite the fact her job was coming to an end and all her chips were down, she still had the grit to work hard right alongside the men. They also had a new respect for the workers after several days of doing the plant workers' jobs. Now they realized how hard everyone worked, each and every day.

19

Change Is In The Air

Elly was finally able to steal away from the grunge table one day and attend to a few things on her desk. Back in the office she came across the letter from the lawyers. In all the excitement, she had forgotten about it. She was very surprised at the letter's contents.

Dear Mrs. Thomas,

We are in the process of probating the will of Samuel S. Dixon and respectfully request your presence in our office soon.

Yours truly,
J.J. O'Malley, Esq.
Barrister and Solicitor

Elly pondered the letter for a few minutes and noted that the date on the letter was almost three weeks earlier. She picked up the telephone and dialed, hoping someone was still there to answer. "Hello, Mr. O'Malley, please."

"Tis I," the male voice responded. "What can I do for you, ma'am?" Although his voice was businesslike, it had a jovial ring to it.

"This is Elspeth Thomas. I realize it's quite late in the day, but I'm responding to your letter dated August 2."

"Mrs. Thomas! I'm glad you finally phoned. I just returned from out of town and was about to call you," he replied. "When can you come to my office? I have something very important to discuss with you. I can't possibly do it over the phone."

"I can come immediately, if that's alright with you."

"That would be wonderful," he replied. "I'm free and at your service. Do you know where we're located?"

"Yes," replied Elly, "I see your address on your letterhead. I used to work for Lamoure's Land Surveying, which is on the same street—at least, it used to be."

"It's still here—a bit of a landmark now," replied O'Malley.

Within minutes, Elly walked into the lawyer's office. Seeing that the receptionist had left for the day, she headed directly to the office with the open door.

Mr. O'Malley pushed back his chair, stood and slowly smiled. He was short, rotund man and appeared far too elderly to still be practicing. From the sound of his voice, Elly had expected someone much younger. He was definitely in his sixties or early seventies, matching the antique furniture of his office. "Please have a chair," he said, gesturing to a vintage padded oak in front of his desk as he in turn seated himself.

"Thank you," replied Elly, following suit. She was anxious to discover what this was all about. She felt filthy from the horrid job and she was hungry. It had been a long day at the count-in table, and she was anxious to return to the comforts of home.

"As I stated in my correspondence, I'm in the process of probating the will of Mr. Samuel Dixon. It is my pleasure, indeed, to advise you that you are the sole beneficiary of his estate."

"Excuse me," replied Elly. "As much as I would love to be someone's beneficiary, I believe you are speaking to the wrong person. I don't know any Mr. Samuel Dixon."

"Well, he certainly knew you! In his will, he states you were always nice to him and brought a lot of sunshine into his life for many years."

"I did?" replied Elly in wonderment. "Who exactly is this Mr. Dixon?"

"You'll probably remember him as the smokies vendor in front of the convention center."

"Oh, you mean Sammy, Sammy with the smokies! After all these years, I didn't even know his last name. He was always just Sammy to me. I enjoyed talking to him on my way into the office each morning. So, Sammy passed away. How sad! I thought he'd just moved to another location. I was sorry we didn't have a chance to say goodbye," she said, feeling an overwhelming sense of loss. "I hope he wasn't sick long. He was such gentle, sweet person. I hope he didn't have to suffer!" Her large eyes welled at the thought of Sammy agonizing for days with a horrible disease, and she dabbed them with tissue. After steadying her emotions, her next thought was, *what on earth would I do with a vending machine?*

"No, he didn't suffer," replied the lawyer, "Thank God for that! He slipped away peacefully in his sleep—his heart just stopped."

Elly was relieved. "I just can't believe Sammy has passed away. He couldn't have been that old," she declared, puzzled. "His registered birth date puts him at seventy-eight—mind you, that's still young nowadays."

"Of course it is," Elly agreed, recognizing the lawyer's sensitivity to his own years. "But really," she continued, "like most gentlemen his age these days, he didn't look a day older than sixty!"

"That's very true," O'Malley said, faking a cough with smiling eyes. *Darn it, anyway, I could talk to her all day!* "Well, I guess we need to get down to the business at hand."

"Quite frankly, Mr. O'Malley, I really can't imagine what I'm going to do with a vending machine, though it was extremely nice of Sammy to think of me."

"Allow me to explain, Mrs. Thomas. Sammy's estate, I mean, Mr. Dixon's estate, is much greater than a mere vending machine." The lawyer went over to the water cooler and brought a glass to Elly. "You may need this," he said with a half smile.

Elly's eyes grew larger, shocking the lawyer, who'd never seen eyes quite so big or so beautiful.

"Although not completely totaled yet, his estate is way up in the millions, maybe billions. As a matter a fact, he's the owner of Summergrove Convention Center Inc. He also owns its subsidiaries, including Sunshine Linen, as well as ten more centers up the coast as far as Oregon and many more in western Canada."

Elly went into a state of shock. Her mouth dried up and she felt the same kind of fright she'd experienced when speaking at Lamoure's farewell. She reached for the glass of water and took a long sip, trying to still her pounding heart. Then she asked the first question that came to mind. "What would possess a millionaire to stand on a street corner selling smokies?" "Wealthy people are often eccentric, Mrs. Thomas. I understand Mr. Dixon sold smokies at each of his centers at one time or another. It was his way of watching his business at work without anyone recognizing him."

"That was clever of him," exclaimed Elly. "But , but doesn't he have a wife or children or other relatives? There has to be someone more important in his life than me."

"No, he is completely without relatives. When he came in to change his will, which had been purely of a charitable nature, he told me you were always kind to him, even gave him part of your office Christmas dinner, and he wanted *you* to be his sole benefactor.

The lawyer stood up to indicate there was no further business to discuss today. "I'm going to need you to sign a lot of papers in due course and will be in touch with you in a few days. I have prepared this letter for you, reaffirming that you are Mr. Dixon's benefactor and new owner of the convention center. In the meantime, drive with caution on the way home. You are in a state of shock. Just think, when you go to the office tomorrow, you'll be working for yourself." He gave a hearty laugh, the sound of which, she was certain, would remain with her a lifetime.

Elly sat there for a minute, trying to digest what had just happened to her and wondering what Vincent would make of it all, before slowly walking out of the lawyer's office. She drove home in a daze, parked with great care in the driveway and mechanically walked up the steps. Her legs felt like wooden stumps.

As she entered, the tantalizing aroma of olive oil, garlic and oregano greeted her. She could hear Vincent in the kitchen preparing dinner. The house felt chilly despite the warmth of the late afternoon. "Hi, dear, I'm home." She shivered. "I'm going to have a quick shower then lie down for a half hour," she called out while laying the car keys on the hall table with a clang . She felt dizzy and, for some reason, frightened.

"Dinner will be ready in about an hour," he called back. "It's your favorite—spaghetti and meatballs." His voice could still boom like a nine-pound hammer.

She skipped the shower and laid on her bed, eyes closed, while the scenario in the lawyer's office played out in her mind over and over again. *What shall I do—what shall I do, oh Lord—what shall I do with all that money?* Her brows knit as she recalled how she and Vincent sometimes would fantasize about winning the lottery. They would laugh and plan how they would spend it. But right now, she couldn't remember what they had eventually decided, not one thing.

Recalling the span of her career and its most memorable segments, she thought about all the people she had encountered in the business world and all their human frailties—and she began to form a plan for how she would spend the money. Rising from the bed, she took a pen and piece of paper from the bureau drawer and began scribbling down her ideas, discovering it is much harder to spend money when you have it than when you don't.

1. Build The Thomas Clinic for the twins at a place of their choice.
2. Build a state-of-the-art retirement home in Summergrove
3. Build an alcohol, drug and tobacco rehabilitation center.
4. Establish a program for single-parent families, summer camp etc.

She paused for a few minutes, pondering what else she would do with her riches. Suddenly, she knew what she would do first: Establish policies and institute changes at Sunshine. This was all she could wrap her mind around for the time being—no doubt she'd think of much more as time passed. For now, she was satisfied that she had determined what to do with at least a small portion of her new riches. After all, from office manager to philanthropist was quite a leap!

She could hear Vincent hard at work, dishes tinkling as he set the table. It was time for dinner and time for her to share the extraordinary events of the day. As the meal concluded, she told Vincent her news. At first he didn't believe her, but when he finally realized it was true, he exclaimed, "It pays to be kind to people, doesn't it, dear?

"Who would have ever imagined when we made the decision for me to go back to work in 1971, it would have come to this."

The look Vincent gave her told her he heard the sentence as she intended.

Contemplating how she would break the news to Hammerstein and the management team, Elly decided to have a little fun with it.

20

The Monumental Effect

The next day, she got up early and spent considerable time with her hair and makeup before donning her very best black suit and red blouse. But this time, her strength came from Sammy, not the colors she wore. It was such a treat to get dressed up again after two weeks of wearing scruffy plant clothes. She arrived at her office well before the picketers and her starting time at the count-in table. She scribbled a quick note to Hammerstein on a post-it note and affixed it to his door:

The owner of Summergrove Convention Center Inc. would like to meet with you and your managers at 9:00 A.M. today for a very important business matter.

When Hammerstein came in and saw the note, he wasn't surprised. The strike had been causing tons of problems for the convention center. He went directly into Elly's office, but surprisingly didn't notice her change of attire. "I want you to clean up the conference room before the owner arrives. And I want you to make coffee, but first I want you to go out and buy a variety of cream donuts—get a large box. You'll have to hurry—there's no time to waste!"

"Do you think one of the guys could go and fetch the donuts? That'll give me more time to tidy up the conference room and make it special."

Her brazen suggestion shocked Hammerstein. *How could she suggest such a ridiculous thing?* He rolled his sappy eyes in exasperation, and then spoke in a much louder tone, one that normally would have offended Elly, but today she was untouchable. "No, that's definitely a woman's job. You'll have plenty time if you hurry. Now, off you go—skedaddle!" He motioned her away as if he were flicking a bug off his clothing.

Elly left quickly to pick up the donuts and then used the next few minutes to tidy the conference room. She had just finished making the coffee and was breathless when they all walked in. Hammerstein was the first to enter, his bottom lip protruding the way it always did when he was worried. Joyble, tall and sleek, followed him. When Jones entered, he looked Elly over with approval. Last to strut in was Malestrom, still wearing the "I want to be company president" look in his eye."

Elly had purposely left the head of the table vacant for the new owner. Everyone took seats at the sides of the table, except Hammerstein, who naturally assumed a seat at the foot, all anxiously waiting for their supreme boss. Finally, Hammerstein lamented, "He should be here by now, damn it all! We've got to get to work. We should phone the airport—maybe his plane was late. Elly, are you sure you got the time right?" Everyone turned to look at Elly accusingly. Finally, Elly stood up and walked around the entire table twice, the second time just for fun, before seating herself squarely in the vacant spot reserved for the owner.

Has the woman lost all her marbles? Completely frustrated by this nonsense, Hammerstein was quick to speak above the snickers coming from the others, "Elly, what on earth do you think you're doing in that chair? You know it's reserved for the owner, if he ever gets here."

"Yes, I know," Elly replied and began giggling devilishly, almost uncontrollably. She was having such a good time!

"Well, then, you should go back to your place, pronto!" he ordered.

"I am in my place!" Elly retorted, her eyes twinkling mischievously and dimples dancing in both cheeks. She saw the impatience in his face quickly turn to anger. He obviously wasn't in the mood for games.

He looked around at the other managers, who now were openly laughing at Elly and her absurd behavior, and stood so abruptly he had to reach back and catch his chair before it fell. "If you don't stop this nonsense, I'm going to have to ask you to leave the room immediately!" he shouted.

"I may have to ask *you* to leave the room," Elly countered and laughed. Not giving him a chance for another threat, she directed her attention to her colleagues. "Well, gentlemen, I do have some news for you all, some great news! " I am the new owner of Summergrove Convention Center Inc. and all its subsidiaries because, you see, I am the sole beneficiary of one Mr. Samuel L. Dixon."

Elly took the letter that clearly stated she was the new owner from her briefcase and passed it across the table, purposely from left to right so it would reach Hammerstein last. She watched Joyble as he read it and could see a vein dancing in his forehead as he nervously drummed his manicured fingers on the table. Elly saw his fright, but he refrained from uttering a word. Jones received the letter next and scanned the single page quickly, then took his time carefully reading it a second time. He turned white as a dove's wing but managed a chuckle and said, "Well, well, I'll be a son of a gun!" She could tell he was shocked but immensely amused. Next, it went to Malestrom, who read and reread it several times. Elly could see the wheels turning in his head as he contemplated how this would affect his getting ahead.

Finally the letter was in Hammerstein's hands. His expression and the way he snatched it indicated his frustration in receiving it last. His jaws kept clamping and unclamping. She also saw that, like Joyble, he feared for his job—when he handed the letter back to Elly, his hand was shaking noticeably and his neck twitched.

If their collective thoughts had been musical instruments when they read the lawyer's letter that spring in the year 2000, from wind to percussion, horns would have blasted while the clang of symbols emanated from Hammerstein. In Elly's mind, however, a flute trilled a sweet melody from a distant hilltop. In her entire life, she'd never heard one more beautiful!

"Does that mean you ... you are now ... now my boss?" Hammerstein squeaked. Oh, how quickly he had humbled!

"That's precisely what it means," Elly declared, unable to disguise the triumph in her voice. She allowed a few moments for them to digest this. When she finally spoke again, her voice had new strength, "First, we put an immediate stop to this ridiculous strike. We give them the money they've demanded and, for good measure, an additional 10 percent retroactive for one year. We all know, after working in the plant for the past two weeks, they deserve every single, measly red penny of it!"

She paused and waited for a response from the men, but got none. The only sound was their breathing and the cries of the picketers outside. She continued, "The accounting function of Sunshine Linen will remain right here in Summergrove, where it belongs. Trying to run an office without its accounts is like trying to drive a truck up a hill sideways without its engine." Her own words made her chuckle softly. "Besides, I have no desire for anyone from any of my corporations to lose their job." Elly's easy use of the word *my* surprised even herself.

"And while we are on the subject of office, gentlemen, I must inform you I'm changing the job title of the computer operator. It's the most complex position in the entire company—a fact that's gone unrecognized for years. Effective today, this position will receive a 30 percent pay hike, retroactive for five years, and will henceforth be called computer data entry specialist.

"Furthermore, there have been and probably still are employees who suffer mental breakdowns. I feel that we, as a company, should make professional help available for these employees. I am hiring a psychologist to be on call—there are exceptional ones both here in California and across the border in British Columbia."

She paused and looked down at her papers then quickly raised her eyes. "There also will be some changes made in management." They all turned and looked at one another, fear of losing their jobs painted all over their faces. "I have established a set of policies for Summergrove Convention Center Inc. and all its subsidiaries to be placed into effect immediately. No, you won't lose your jobs. Thank God, I wasn't raised to hold grudges. But there will be policies established a whole long list of policies, which will be strictly enforced."

She saw relief on their faces and withdrew a sheaf of papers she'd drawn up at sunrise from her briefcase and passed a page to each. "I would like to touch upon just a few, just a few, of these policies. First, should there be women on the management team, they will have wage parity to their male counterparts, receiving the same respect and benefits. Women have joined the corporate workforce, not to be above or below their male counterparts but equal in every way—definitely not handmaidens. You men have to do away with your kitchen mentalities when it comes to your fellow female worker and recognize the equality of women. In that vein, everyone will take a turn making coffee and tidying up the boardroom. And everyone will take a turn staffing the office at lunchtime. Women enjoy having lunch together too, occasionally.

"Furthermore, like his or her colleagues, the office manager, whether a man or a woman, will be replaced when on vacation. This will allow more than ten consecutive days of vacation, with no undue burden upon them on returning. And individual union members shall never be encouraged to apply for a managerial position. This only creates false hopes and grave disappointments. She turned her gaze to Joyble, who knew Elly was thinking of Carlita and flinched.

"And paid sick leave will go into effect immediately for all managers. No one should face the trauma of an illness and lack of money at the same time. Now, lack of strict adherence to the next policy will be just cause for instant dismissal. At no time shall a manager use rank to exercise power over a subordinate to obtain undue advantage for himself." She swung her piercing gaze once again toward Joyble, who flinched again.

"Now, if you all want to keep your positions, you'll follow these company policies faithfully. Trust me, I'll have a way of knowing if you don't. In addition, I'm asking one final and very important thing of you all. You must keep my ownership a secret. You may think it's foolish, but no one must ever know. You can consider that a threat, as well as a request. I want to retire from my position and walk out the front door as Elly the office manager. Have I made myself clear?"

Looking at each one, she received their gaping nods. "Oh, one more thing—I'll be retiring from my position immediately." Smiling, she turned to Hammerstein and spoke with a new authority, "Start looking for a replacement at once, please." She wanted to finish with "skedaddle," but rose above it. "You know what has to be done, George, and what's needed to accomplish it. So, please get the show on the road as quickly as you can." She got up, squared her shoulders and, with head held high, headed toward the office, leaving the men behind to discuss their new situation.

Back at her desk, she paused for a few moments and gazed out her window at the strikers. She saw Hammerstein approaching the union president, who then dispersed the picketers and followed Hammerstein into the boardroom to sign the new contract, which would bring all the employees back to their jobs in the morning.

Within a few days, the hum of the plant and office was back to normal, but with the strike over and a raise in the offing, there was a new energy among the employees. Just before lunch, Elly announced to her staff, "Come on, ladies, I want to take you for pizza. Let's celebrate the new contract. I know you all like pizza and it's an all-you-can-eat deal. Walter's agreed to watch the office for us."

While munching on pizza, they talked about what was happening in the office—how the accounts were staying in Summergrove and the pay raise—and they wondered how it was all going to turn out once Elly left. Elly listened with a smile. Hammerstein had posted her retirement on the bulletin board in the hallway for everyone to see. "We're going to really miss you, Elly," Rita said. "I can't imagine the office without you. You gave it class, honest, you did."

"You got that right, Rita!" Melody said and giggled. "We'll really miss you. As a matter of fact, I think I shall cry when you leave. I think I shall blubber all over town." She avoided Elly's eyes.

"I'll miss you both, too!" replied Elly. "We've come a long way together—shared so much! You women have worked hard, and I've appreciated you both more than words can ever say. We've had the most efficient office in the entire corporation for years. In addition, we collected all the money. As I see it, Melody, you and Rita will work happily together for many years. You both will be just fine! Just remember, life is a process of constant change. We must flow with the tide. Everyone has to adapt to the changing times and march into the twentieth century in tune with the world."

"But I hate change! I hate it like a bad toothache," said Melody, her face showing real concern. "I hated the computer when it first came in, and I hate the thought of you leaving now." She averted her eyes and picked up a large piece of pizza from the platter.

"Me, too," said Rita, her brown eyes welling up behind her glasses. "I'm going to bawl like hell when you leave."

"Well," said Elly with tongue in cheek, "when I leave, I want you both to do more than cry. I want you to wail! Do you hear? I mean really wail." She paused and feigned the sound of a coyote in the back of her throat. "Wailing is most effective—it's what convinced Vincent to agree to my returning to work way back when. I was good at it." *But you don't have to break any hairbrushes,* she thought. Elly's attempt to turn a sad moment into one of humor seemed to work—they all were laughing now.

Elly thanked her staff again for helping collect the past due accounts, and Rita and Melody for helping with Lamoure's farewell party and, most of all, for being her friends. She exclaimed, "What a beautiful way to end my career! By helping so vigilantly, you ladies allowed me to finish on a positive note—that was important to me."

Hammerstein was pleased about that, too, extremely pleased—it drew compliments from his superiors in head office about his management skills. He was also pleased about something else—he was being transferred back to the Big Apple. If he'd thought about it a while, he would have guessed that Elly had orchestrated it. With Hammerstein's position up for grabs, Elly could give eager young Malestrom his chance. Anyone wanting to climb the corporate ladder as badly as he did deserved it. They decided to keep his promotion a secret, too, for now.

Realizing a farewell party for Elly would be required, Hammerstein called Rita and Melody into his office to make arrangements.

The party was held at popular restaurant, the more than fifty people squeezed into its back room. Rita and Melody had decorated the room beautifully with balloons, flowers and a big heart-shaped sign wishing her well. The speeches were all touching, and she loved the gift of luggage and gold watch from the company—more accurately, from herself.

How did these past twenty-eight years—eleven with Lamoure's and seventeen with Sunshine—evaporate so quickly? It all seemed like a dream, now, a small chunk of time filled to the brim with memories to take into retirement. She thought of all the different personalities she had encountered over the years, the human frailties she had witnessed. And she thought about the remarkable courage she'd seen in others when the chips were down.

Now that Elly could think of Hammerstein as an employee rather than a boss, her opinion of him changed. Despite everything, she had to admire him—he'd had the courage to make staff changes and he'd maintained the company through the strike. Although Elly hadn't always agreed with the way he had done things, it didn't matter now. Her new policies would circumvent changes. And if what he'd done for Crowfoot turned out well, everything else was inconsequential.

As for Billington, perhaps he'd be able to use the same cunning he'd used to walk down the wrong road to now turn his life around. One could only hope—there's always hope. At any rate, Elly's new treatment center would soon become a reality. It would offer help to him and others like him. She would find ways of seeking him out and encouraging him.

Life had taught her not to judge people too quickly—appearances can be deceiving and first impressions illusionary. Time is the best adjudicator of people. It always has been and always will be. And to really know someone takes two years. Now, as she thought about it all, she focused on only good things, the positive things. Vincent had taught her and the twins to do that—something he had so much trouble practicing himself.

She also thought about all the changes in the business world during this last third of the twentieth century. Her career had seen many. She thought about how strange it was to be addressing one another by first names rather than using the formal Mr. and Mrs. and how unconventional office attire had become. She thought about the technological advances—high-tech calculators, fax machines, cell phones, photocopiers that count and sort—and, most of all, the computer and its amazing Internet. She wondered what could possibly be next.

Human sensibilities had changed, too, or perhaps people had become more broad minded about morality and its definition. She thought about Vincent and how he had hated to see her leave the house for the business world. His fears had finally left him but now, in retrospect, he was right about so many things.

She thought about how difficult it had been at first when she went back to work and how Vincent had overcome his objections and supported her. And how quickly her sons adapted—learning how to do their own laundry, sew on a button and cook a simple meal by the time they were twelve! Contemplating her career and her life on her very last day at the office, Elly also realizes her mother was right—the greatest job anyone will ever have is raising a child. Children are a process and always a privilege. A job goes, but a child is forever!

Yes, there was change in her future. Retirement was going to be a new dance, but she was looking forward to it. She knew she'd have no problem learning the steps—why, she might even invent a few of her own. Now that wealth had been bestowed upon her, there was so much to plan, build and do. There were so many people needing help!

On the last day of her working career, she struggled to keep busy. It was a day without a long to-do list, a day of not really doing very much at all, just tidying up her desk and files and preparing a box of personal items to take home. The florist brought in a dozen yellow roses, another gift from the corporation. And a single red rose arrived with a card that read, "Hurry home! Love, Vincent."

She planned to leave at two that afternoon—they all knew it—and everyone seemed to be hanging around when she finally headed for her car. Like an entourage, they all marched out with her, all the men she'd worked alongside during the strike and Rita on her right and Melody on left, just like a herd of elephants guarding a newborn. It was surreal!

It also was bizarre that Elly, who by nature was sentimental and cried at the slightest hint of pathos, now at the end of her career had eyes as dry as the Mojave. As her fellow workers all lined up by her car to hug and wish her well, one by one explaining how they'd miss her, she was engulfed by a sensation of complete elation. Sammy's generosity had given her the ability to help others in the future, and giving joy to others was the real joy in having 'real' money.

As she backed out of the parking lot where she'd waited all those years earlier for that very important interview, she saw her co-workers waving. She smiled, waved back and blew them a kiss, failing to notice that Rita and Melody were no longer present. They had hurried in the side door and through the office, down the long, odorous hallway and across the fancy lobby to stand on the steps of the front entrance to the convention center. Luckily, she happened to glance in their direction as she drove by, otherwise she might never had seen their charming little gesture. Each was holding the corner of a large towel and rubbing her eyes.

200

Exactly as she had requested when they were eating pizza, they were wailing!

She tooted the horn three times in response and thought, *They are going to be two very surprised ladies when they arrive home today! I'd love to see their expressions when they see cars from an anonymous donor sitting in their driveways, all shiny and new. I'd love to see their happy faces!*

She drove slowly with her window down, hugging the California shoreline and savoring the white-capped blue waters and shrimp-scented air. Seagulls swirled low, while a bald eagle soared high overhead. *A good omen,* she thought. *The eagle is Vincent's favorite bird—he says it has a wingspan of six feet. .*

Many years later, an elderly lady in shabby clothes can be seen outside Sunshine Linen, selling smokies. Her smile flashes a dimple, and if one looks closely, a few remnants of red tinges her silver hair. *Aw Shoot!!!!!*